My Life

As I Remember It

Oak of Acadiana Publications
18896 Greenwell Springs RD
Greenwell Springs, LA 70739
www.thepublishedword.com

I0155381

My Life

As I Remember It

by

Teddie Irwin

Published by:

Oak of Acadiana Publications
18896 Greenwell Springs Road
Greenwell Springs, LA 70739
www.thepublishedword.com

ISBN 978-1-934769-32-4

Printed on Demand in the US and the UK
For Worldwide Distribution

Dedication

To my children, with love, for being who you are,
independent, strong and caring adults. You are
always there when I need you, and I am very
proud of each of you. You treat me like a queen,
and a mother could not ask for anything more.

Acknowledgments

I am grateful for anyone and everyone who has helped me along life's way, and there have been many. In each life, angels come and go when you need them, and I've had my share, too many to name. But if you are reading this, you know who you are.

I do need to name a few:

Elmer and Patty Kibbie, both now gone. Such dear friends!

Last, but not least, **Mary Lou Lemond** and **Velma Richard**. These two women helped me in so many ways. I could never thank them enough for being in my life.

The Poems

The two poems that follow have meant a lot to me throughout the years. I have kept them close at hand and read them almost daily. The one is printed out and hangs in my dressing room. The other is hand lettered and hangs in my office. I am grateful to the poets who penned them, for their words have gotten me through many difficult days and continue to be a blessing to me each and every day.

After A While
By Veronica A. Shoffstall

After a while …
You learn the subtle difference
between holding a hand and chaining a soul
And you learn that love doesn't mean leaning,
and company doesn't always mean security.
And you begin to learn that kisses aren't contracts
and presents aren't always promises
And you begin to accept your defeats
with your head up and your eyes ahead,
with the grace of a woman, not the grief of a child.
And you learn to build all your roads on today
because tomorrow's ground is too uncertain,
for plans and futures have a way of falling down
in mid-flight.
After a while, you learn that even sunshine burns
if you get too much.
So you plant your own garden
and decorate your own soul
instead of waiting for someone to bring you flowers
And you learn that you really can endure,
that you really are strong,
and you really do have worth,
And you learn and you learn.
With every good-bye, you learn.

The Man Who Thinks He Can
by Walter D. Wintle

If you think you're beaten, you are;
If you think you dare not, you don't.
If you'd like to win, but think you can't,
It's almost a cinch you won't.

If you think you'll lose, you've lost;
For out of the world we find
Success being with a fellow's will;
It's all in the state of mind.

If you think you're outclassed, you are;
You've got to think high to rise.
You've got to be sure of yourself
Before you can win a prize.

Life's battles don't always go
To the stronger or faster man;
But soon or late, the one who wins
Is the man who thinks he can.

Contents

Introduction

For a long while now I have had the sense that I must take the time and make the effort to write down some memories of my life for the sake of coming generations. I tried to start several times, and I found the going very difficult—for several reasons:

1. How do you capture eighty years of life on the few pages of a book?
2. Memories are funny things. Two people who have had the very same experience often remember it differently. This shows us clearly

that memories are subject to our interpretation.

3. Much of what I remembered, especially from my early life, seemed sad, and I didn't want to just write a woe-is-me report. That wouldn't help anyone.

4. As we age, memories are one of the many things we often start to lose, especially the detail of them.

Still, I knew that I must write my story. All I can tell you is that this is how I remember my life. And, in the end, I found that I had to tell the story, whether it was sometimes sad or not. Along with any sadness, I can also tell you that trials and difficulties build character in us, when we learn to face them squarely and keep moving forward toward a better future for ourselves and others. This is my fervent wish for my children and grandchildren and each succeeding generation.

Teddie Irwin
Carencro, Louisiana

Chapter 1

My Entrance into This World

I came into this world on October 21, 1929 in Cleveland, Ohio, during what proved to be a very difficult time for this country and the whole world, the beginnings of what we now call the Great Depression. Why I was born in Cleveland I never knew, except that my birth certificate shows that my father was a cab driver in that city. His name was Chester Burgher. Where my mother met this man and why she went to Ohio in the first place I have also never known.

What is known is that Mother, Laurel Mabel Cavalier, was just twenty-one at the time and far from home. She and my father were not married, and how long their relationship lasted or how long she remained in Cleveland I cannot say. In time, we went back to New Orleans, and that's where I grew up, with no memories of Ohio or my father. He, therefore, has remained a mystery to me most of my life.

I was always taught to spell our family name as Burgher, although the person who filled out my birth certificate spelled it Berger. Later research revealed that Chester Burgher was originally from Vancouver, Canada, where many Germans had settled—among them a large colony of Burghers. After arriving in the New World, the Burghers dropped the Von from their surname, but various spellings of it developed, and, through the years this complicated any search for my father.

My earliest memories are of Mother and myself living with a lady named Ma Pool in New Orleans. This lady ran a boarding house there, and for some reason, we lived with her in several different locations at several different intervals. Each of her boarders had a private bedroom, and Ma Pool cooked for everyone.

Those boarding house were interesting places. Life, in those days, was not anything like it is today. Nowadays everyone has their own living room, bedroom, kitchen and bathroom, but it was not so then. In those widely-used boarding houses, many times there was only one bathroom, and everyone had to use it. We are indeed a blessed people today.

Ma Pool also "looked after" me when Mother was at work, but she was not a very loving person, and my memory is that I spent most of my time trying to find ways to entertain myself.

I'm not sure what my mother's education was, but in that time most women had very little education, and it was not an easy time for anyone to find a job. For the first ten or twelve years of my life, Mother made her living as a dime-a-dance girl, doing just what the name suggests. The problem was that the atmosphere in which the dancing took place was not always very good, and my mother always had to work nights. So each evening I was left alone. There were other people in the house, but I had no real companionship or guidance.

Mother often drank and came home only in the wee hours of the morning. What's worse, when she did come home, she wanted to vent her frustrations on someone, and often she woke me up, and I had to listen to things that no small child should ever have to hear, let alone a girl of my age. The next day she slept late, and I was on my own again. There were no other children around, and the adults who were around didn't seem to have time for me, so my days seemed very long and lonely.

Again, that's how I remember it, and I'm very willing to admit that my memory may not be totally accurate. But I can only tell what I remember. All in all, it was not a very auspicious beginning for life.

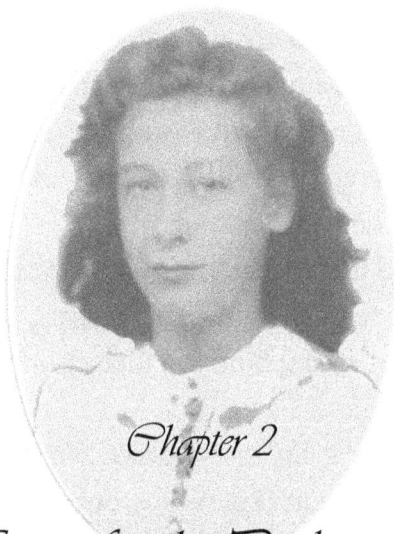

Chapter 2

Our Family Background

The Cavaliers, my mother's family, were a mix of French and Italian heritage, and then my father added in the German, so what was I?

My grandmother, Sarah (Frazand) Cavalier, or Mère as we knew her, was born in Sicily and immigrated to the United States. Her husband, Richard Cavalier (Père), who died when I was about three, came here from France. Together they had eight children—three boys and five girls.

The oldest boy was also named Richard, next came

Gerald, and the youngest son was Octavia. The girls were Catherine, Laurel, Margaret, Helen and Hazel. This was the world into which I was born.

Uncle Gerald had one daughter, Aunt Catherine had one daughter, Laurel (my mother) had two children—one boy and one girl, and Aunt Helen also had two children—a boy and a girl. Neither Aunt Margaret nor Aunt Hazel had any children.

It was said that Richard moved to Alaska. He would show up periodically through the years, and someone would report seeing him, but little else was known of his personal life.

Octavia, Uncle Tay, as we called him, was different. At the time, we didn't know why, but now I understand that he was gay. He was also the outlaw of the family and seemed to be always in and out of jail, mainly because he drank a lot down in the French Quarter, and that got him into trouble. On occasion, we saw him, but we were never close to him. Uncle Jerry was the one we saw more often. He was a very sweet man.

Uncle Jerry's wife was named Emily, and their daughter was named Jackie (Jacqueline). Aunt Helen married a Lacoste and had two children, Milton and Shirley. They were to be the closest of my cousins, and we're still close today. Milton and Shirley now live in Metarie, Louisiana.

Catherine's daughter was named Dorothy, and we called her Googie. Unfortunately, Googie passed away in her early forties from cancer. Laurel, of course, had the two of us, Teddie and Terry, and, as you will see, we attempted to make the best life possible for ourselves.

Chapter 3

My Own Little Person

I felt very alone in this world ... until the day my brother Terry came along, and then I had him. I was ten at the time.

Terry was my own little person, and I treasured him. We did everything together, despite the difference in age. That was the best of times in my young life, as far as I was concerned.

Terry's father (for whom he was named) worked for the railroad, handling the U.S. Mail, and because of that, although he lived in Texas, he often travelled to New Orleans, and there he met my mother. They married, and we moved to Houston to be closer to his work. In Houston, we had a real house, a very nice house in a very nice neighborhood.

Things were much better for us in other ways. Mother didn't have to work, so she was home with us and seemed to be happier. Life was less stressful for her, and so she drank less, and that made life a whole lot better for me and my new baby brother. At last, it seemed, we would live as a real family ought to.

But it was not to be. Our "father" was often not at home, and whether or not Mother learned the truth about his double life or not I can't be sure, but, before too long, he was not coming home at all. Not too long after Terry was born, we moved back to New Orleans, and our life returned to its former cadence, except that now I had someone to share my loneliness and someone to take care of.

I don't remember us taking any furniture with us to Houston. Was it a furnished house we lived in there? Did we take anything with us when we left to go back to New Orleans? Did we have pieces of furniture stored somewhere in New Orleans that we retrieved when we got back home? How long were we actually in Houston? Unfortunately, I have no answers to these questions. I don't remember, and everyone else involved has long ago passed on.

In later years, my brother discovered that while his father was married to our mother, he was also married to another woman in Texas. They had no children, but apparently he was a bigamist.

Although Terry Sr. and Mother divorced, he didn't totally disappear from our lives. It seems that he still came around or contacted Mother in some way because occasionally we heard from him. He showed up once when Terry had to be hospitalized for a serious infection in his ankle bone and again at my wedding years later. But he was, for all practical purposes, an absentee father, and so neither Terry nor I had the benefit of a father's wisdom or guidance as we grew up. This man may have helped pay the hospital expenses on that one occasion, but I feel confident that he never sent my mother any regular child support. We never saw any of it if he did.

That short stay in Houston, in some ways, seemed like a fairy tale. There were children next door I could play with, and for the first time, we were not in a boarding house or tiny apartment, and for the first time we had a sense of family.

I remember only one other house that we lived in through the years, and our stay there was not a long one. It was a small shotgun house on Maurepas Street in New Orleans. For some reason, a woman named Rose lived with us there. It was a duplex, and someone lived next door. My memories of that house are fleeting, probably because our stay there was just as fleeting. From there we went on to live in several apartments, and then we moved in with Mère.

Chapter 4

Terry Was My Responsibility

Mother was working again, and Terry was basically my responsibility. He always said in later life that the way he was as an adult was the way I taught him as a child: to keep his clothes clean and his shoes polished and to present himself well. I ironed his clothes before he went to school. I took him to school. I picked him up after school, and then he and I would be by ourselves until Mother came home at night. Because of this, the two of us were very close. Of course, as I noted, I was ten years older than he, so, in many ways, I was more like a mother to him than a sister. What is sure is that life was very hard for the both of us. The times when we were able to stay together were the best of those bad times, but sometimes, for reasons that we could never understand or that were never explained to us, we were separated. I was sent to one aunt to live, and Terry was sent to another. Where our mother was during these times we never knew. Whether it was an economic move or something else, we had no idea. We did what we were told to do, and we learned that we obeyed the person whose roof we were under at the moment.

Some of the saddest words I ever remember hearing in life were "You can't stay here anymore," and we heard them quite a few times, but what could we do? We moved so often and never had any place to call our own, so what was one more move? We sucked in our emotions and gathered together our meager belongings to transfer to the next "home."

Why I had to stay with Aunt Helen and Terry had to stay with Aunt Catherine I never knew. I assumed that Mother just didn't have money to feed us. When she could, she came and got us, and we would be together again—for a while. But nothing was guaranteed. While staying with Aunt Catherine, Terry had a very hard time. She'd had a hard life herself, and was very bitter about it, so she took it out on others. Terry suffered her wrath many times.

Wherever we happened to be staying, an attempt was always made to get us all together for Sunday dinner. Sometimes it was at Mère's house, sometimes at Aunt Helen's house and, more rarely, at Aunt Catherine's house. One Sunday we all ate at Aunt Catherine's, and as Aunt Helen and I were leaving I was torn up emotionally because I knew Terry was having a hard time. Aunt Catherine was being so very mean to him, and I didn't want to leave him there alone with her. But we had no choice in the matter. Thank God he survived.

When Terry was about three, we were back living with Ma Pool, and Mother was working nights as usual. Ma Pool's house, this time, was in Gentilly, not far from the railroad tracks, and every day she would cook lunch for the railroad workers, and they would walk the block or so through the field to her house to eat. There was a hole in the roof of that house, and each night, as we lay in bed, we could see the stars. Now that seems so very primitive, but we didn't think anything of it in those days. Children are resilient, and they can bear a lot and bounce back.

Ma Pool had moved several times, and we had

moved much more. I can't remember where that first house was. The two I remember were the one on Burgundy Street right off of Esplanade (we lived there several times) and the one just off of Gentilly Highway.

Things improved when I was thirteen. Mother changed jobs and started working in a restaurant, so now she could be home at night. We lived in a series of small apartments, somewhere she could walk to the streetcar and get her ride to work.

When we moved to Carondalet Street, Terry and I would ride the St. Charles streetcar, then transfer to the Esplanade bus, and I would take him to Mc-Donald Elementary School, and I would walk back three blocks to my all-girl school, John McDonough High. In the afternoons, the process was reversed. I walked over and picked him up from school, and then we caught the bus and transferred to the street car to get back home. You can't spend that much time together without becoming close, and we were close.

Chapter 5

Our Last Moves as a Family

Before high school, I had attended so many different schools that I lost count, so when I started high school, I determined that I would stay in the same school, no matter where or how often we moved. I didn't care how many buses or street cars I had to ride to get there. I would finish in the same school I had started in. Thankfully, I was able to keep that determination. No matter where we lived in the New Orleans area, I got to school. If it took me an hour or even two hours, and I had to transfer several times, I did it.

High school was very enjoyable for me. I made friends in the classroom, but, for the most part, we had very little interaction outside of that context. I didn't want most of the other young people to know where I lived or how I lived. They lived with a family, and I did not. They had a home, and I did not. I didn't want these facts to be known.

There were a few exceptions. Prominent among them were Lilly Mae Blanchard and Anna Mae Smith. They were my dancing buddies in school, drawn together because we were so alike. Lilly lived with her aunt, and Anna Mae lived with her grandparents. In our junior and senior years the three of us went to Mardi Gras together and had a great time.

Lois Dorch and I were also dancing buddies. Sometimes I would spend Friday night at her home, and her mother would drop us off at the docks, where "The President" (a paddle-wheel boat) was docked. It was a place we could go and dance. The boat would leave the dock at 9 in the evening and return at midnight, and her mom would pick us up. Saturday morning Lois and I would walk together through the French Quarter. That was a great time for both of us.

Years later, when Andy, my oldest dauther, was about three years old, I was out walking with my girls, Andy and Lillian, one day and ran into Lilly. As it turned out, she lived just a few blocks from us. We saw each other for a while before we moved again. Wherever we went, Lilly and I kept in touch, and through the years we saw each other every now and then. When we left Thibodaux, we stayed with her and her family in Kentwood until we could find a house in Houston. That was a bittersweet time for both of us. Lilly passed away some years later of cancer. It's funny how some things still hurt after all the years have passed.

During those high school years, there were very few other outside activities because, first of all, we had no money for it. I remember bowling on a few occasions and very occasionally seeing a movie. But that was the extent of our outside activities. Life was hard.

During my senior year of high school, Mother, Terry and I lived with Mère. She was working for a man whose wife had died, leaving him with two children to care for, and then he developed TB. It was mandatory in those days for TB sufferers to be institutionalized in a sanitarium, so his family paid Mère to stay in the house and care for the children, and she asked us to move in there and help her, and we did.

As the school year came to a close, I needed a graduation dress, an evening gown, and there was no way we could afford one, so Mother stopped smoking long enough to save money to buy me the dress. It was a rare sacrifice. She had been smoking for as long as I could remember (and she went right back to it as soon as the dress was bought).

For the most part, I did well in high school, but I had an English teacher named Miss McGruder, and her room was always much too warm for my tastes. No sooner would I walk into her classroom than I started coughing, and she would give me dirty looks, as if I could stop the coughing at will. It got to the place that whenever I started coughing, she would send me out into the hall, and I would sit there on the steps until the bell rang for the next class. Amazingly, no other teacher or principle ever came along and saw me sitting there on the steps during English class. Maybe that explains why I'm not the best when it comes to correct grammar.

My only real interest outside of school was reading. Like most girls in those days, I worked to master things like sewing and crocheting. For a long time, however, I did entertain the idea of becoming a doctor. All thoughts of that flew away when I was suddenly swept off my feet by a man.

Chapter 6

My Spiritual Formation

Before I get to the romance part, let me mention something about my spiritual roots. The Cavaliers were Catholic, and as far back as I can remember, Mother made sure I went to services at a local Catholic church every week, as there was usually one within walking distance of us. But I went alone; she never went with me.

During my high school years, I got up my nerve to tell Mother that I was no longer satisfied with the Catholic Church and wanted to find something more personally fulfilling. She agreed, but I would have to find a new church on my own. In the process, I attended services with the Jehovah's Witnesses, the Baptists, the Methodists and others. Eventually I settled on the Methodist Church.

Mère, for one, was not happy with this decision. She had been a staunch Catholic her whole life and was sure that no one could go to Heaven if they were not Catholic.

Fortunately, when I met a man and fell in love, he, too, was a Methodist, and we agreed to raise our children as Methodists, so my newfound faith did not present a conflict there.

Chapter 7

Swept Off My Feet

Soon after I graduated from high school, we moved again, this time to a second-floor apartment on the corner of Carondolet Street, not far from St. Charles. It was actually a boarding house run by a woman named Lillian Sewell. Her son had just come home from the war and had been on Iwo Jima when the famous flag was raised there. His name was Nemour Clemont Fourroux, Jr., and everyone called him Junior. Being around Junior was a totally new experience for me. I had never dated and had attended an all-girl high school, so I wasn't accustomed to being around boys. He was extremely intelligent, witty and charming, and he quickly swept me off my feet.

Soon after we moved to that place, two memorable things happened: One of the famous hurricanes of the time struck (known in history simply as the Hurricane of 1947), and I got my first job, working in an office downtown. My second day on the job, a fat man called me into his office and said to me, "Look, I want you to go out and buy some red lipstick and wear it. I don't like women who don't wear lipstick." There was another girl working there, but I had a very funny feeling about that man and his intentions He gave me the heebie-jeebies, so I quit the job. Fortunately, I was able to find another one within a few days, and went to work for a finance company. But I had other things on my mind.

Just released from the Marine Corps, Junior had fought in far-flung places for the past four years, and he was three years older than I. I, therefore, considered him to be a man of the world and was quickly taken with him. Mother didn't like him at all, calling him "a guttersnipe." The feeling was mutual. He didn't like her either.

Junior and I began dating, and he very quickly

asked me to marry him. It was so sudden and out in left field that I answered him jokingly, "Oh, yes. I'll marry you on Christmas Eve." Well, all jokes aside, we did get married on Christmas Eve 1947. I had just met him in August of the year before.

The ceremony took place at 8th Street Methodist Church at an 8 o'clock PM service. Aunt Margaret and her husband, Uncle Lenny, came from Mobile to be with us for the occasion, and he gave me away. As I noted earlier, Terry's father popped in for the ceremony. He must have been in town anyway and heard about the wedding. I never knew for sure.

We spent that first night of our married life at Mother's apartment and, after having Christmas dinner with her the next day, we boarded a Grey-hound bus for Jena, Louisiana, to spend the rest of our honeymoon in the home of Junior's aunt and uncle, his mother's sister and her husband. We called them Aunt Berta and Uncle T.E. (his name was Truman).

Junior loved that place in Jena because it was in the country and had wonderful hunting and fishing. The trip there was beautiful because: (1) We were so in love, and (2) Much of the ride was at night, and everyone had their Christmas lights on.

When we arrived in Jena, someone picked us up

and took us to the home of Aunt Berta and Uncle T.E. I couldn't tell much about it that night except that it was out in the country with nothing else around. It was embarrassing for me to be in a strange house, having been married just one day, but everyone made me feel right at home.

For a New Orleans girl, life in Jena was a shock. The house had no running water and no inside bathroom. They did have lights and a telephone (because Uncle T.E. worked for the phone company.) What amazed me most was the amount of food that was prepared and served each day. Breakfasts were huge, and lunches were even bigger. There were several kinds of meats and fresh vegetables, and plenty of fresh biscuits and corn bread. At supper time, we ate the abundant leftovers from lunch.

Junior was bound and determined to take me hunting while we were there, but I wasn't so sure. I had never held a gun in my hands. He patiently taught me how to shoot a shotgun and also a 22 caliber pistol. We went fishing and searching for arrowheads. This was so different from anything I had ever done before, and I loved it. In the future, we went back to Jena as often as we could, and when the children came along, they loved Jena as much as we did.

Back in New Orleans, we found a small apartment near Mother and lived there for a short time
while Junior looked for a job. In the process of job
hunting, he heard about an opportunity to enter
a totally new field—television. United Television
Laboratories was inviting recruits to study the new
technology in their school in Louisville, Kentucky.
Junior had been a communications specialist in the
military, and everyone called him "Sparky." He was
very excited about this idea, but I wasn't so sure.
Here I was, eighteen years old, newly married,
and now we had to pick up everything and move
to another state. I had thought that once we were
married, life would totally change. Well, in some
ways, it changed, but in other ways, it seemed to
stay the same. We were moving again.

Chapter 8

The Fourroux Family

Before I tell you about Louisville, let me say a few words about the Fourroux family. I don't know all there is to know about the family, but I do know that Junior was born in New Orleans, as was his father before him. The family, at some point, had immigrated to New Orleans from Paris, France. Unlike many of the Cajun families of Louisiana that received their French heritage from the mass expulsion of French-speaking people from Canada, Junior's line was more direct. In fact,

Nemour is the name of a section of Paris, as Andy noticed the last time she was there.

His mother's name was Lillian Mae. Nemour Sr. and Lillian had four children, two boys and two girls: Nemour Jr., Norville, Hazel and Betty.

Betty married Jimmy Sloan and had five children. They lived in Ohio, so we never knew them well.

Hazel had only one child, Charles. We called him Champ. He lived in Florida.

Norville and his wife had five boys: Truman (T.E.), Norville Jr., Dale, Frank and Leslie. Frank and Leslie were twins, and Leslie died at six weeks of age.

Junior and I went on to have five girls, as I will relate in time.

At one point, when the Fourroux children were still small, Lillian contracted TB (or, at least, was thought to have contracted it) and had to be placed in a sanitarium. Junior's father, not knowing how to care for the children, sent them to an orphanage, where they lived for about a year. Fortunately, Lillian was released from the sanitarium, and they resumed their life together. She was a nurse, but I'm not sure if she was a nurse before she was hospitalized or became one afterward.

After Nemour Sr. left her and married their maid, she remarried, to Leslie Sewell, a chemist for the State of Louisiana.

Well, I had married young into a family of French heritage and was eager to see what life had in store for me. At the moment, I was on my way to Kentucky.

Chapter 9

Life in Louisville

At first, moving to Louisville did not seem to be such a dramatic change. There were lots of apartments there, and they seemed to be much like the apartments we'd had in New Orleans. But it didn't take long for me to begin to discover some differences.

For example, I was shocked the first time I rode a public bus to see that whites and blacks sat together. In New Orleans, the blacks were still riding at the back of the bus.

The food was also very different that far north, and my neighbors were surprised by what we ate. The only friends we developed while we were there were neighbors, and then only to say hello. We moved too much to make strong or lasting friendships.

To support us while he went to school, Junior loaded a milk truck at night and then went to school during the day. None of the places we lived in was very close to his school, so he always had to take a bus.

Loading milk trucks soon got old, and he found a job as a night desk clerk at a hotel. That was better. Later, another hotel offered him a job, as well as a place for us to stay, so that helped us a lot. He was the night desk clerk, and was also responsible for stoking the furnace before going to school each day that winter. I helped to support us by cleaning rooms.

It was a rough time, and this was complicated, when, while we were living in Louisville, our first child was born. It was March 10, 1949. We named her Andrea Louise and called her Andy or Andy Lou. Because she was our first child, both of us doted on her, but she was the apple of her father's eye. The name Andrea had been his idea. I'd never heard it before, but he had and he loved it. The middle name, Louise, was after his grandmother.

We felt like we could endure the loneliness and strangeness of Louisville, because Junior was getting a good education in a promising field. Surely our future would be secure. Or so we thought anyway.

Our next child was also born there in Louisville on July 23, 1950, just as Junior was finishing his schooling and preparing to take his first job, in Bloomington, Indiana. We named her Lillian Ann, after his mother. When Lillian came along, we were living in a third-floor apartment. The bathroom was on the second floor, and if you wanted to wash clothes, you had to go to the machine in the basement. So you carried your dirty clothes down several flights of stairs and then carried the clean clothes back up after washing them.

When Junior left for Bloomington and I was left alone there with two babies, it was the only time in my life that I ever had a diaper service. I had to do it. Andy was less than two years old and Lillian was a newborn.

It was hard enough just surviving. I had just had a baby, but I had to go down to the second floor to use the bathroom and down to the basement to do the laundry. Fortunately, there was a very nice lady, who was either the landlady or the superintendent of the apartment building, and she took pity on us and would come up and help me. Sometimes she took the wet clothes and hung them out on the line to dry. I was grateful to her. I needed all the help I could get.

Chapter 10

On to Bloomington

Junior had graduated with honors, completing a four-year college course in just two years. With everything else that was going on, it was a laudable feat.

Then, very quickly, he was hired by RCA. But they needed him in Bloomington, Indiana, and, at the moment, we couldn't afford to take the whole family (and I was nearing the delivery date with Lillian), so it was decided that he would leave us in Louisville, go alone to Bloomington to start the job, and we would follow later.

In Bloomington, he found a nice second-floor apartment that the family of one of his fellow workers had and was able to rent it for himself. Later, we all lived there.

Before he could leave for Bloomington, Lillian was born. He took me home from the hospital, and then he had to leave for Indiana because he had to report for work the very next day. For the next six weeks, the girls and I had to fend for ourselves. When Lillian was six weeks old, and we considered that she was doing well enough for us all to travel, Junior came back and got us, and we all moved to Bloomington.

Bloomington was a very nice town, but not having a car, I really didn't get to see much of it. We moved there in August, and it was already getting cool at night, and when winter set in with a vengeance, we were stuck inside. That year, the temperature plunged to twenty below zero, and the girls and I would sit in the warmth of the kitchen looking out at all the snow.

I had to walk to the store when a neighbor was available to watch the girls during their nap times. Bloomington was hilly, and those hills were now slippery. I remember one particular day having to finally struggle up the hill on my knees after slipping and sliding around for a while with my grocery bags. All in all, it was a lot for a Southern girl.

Chapter 11

Moving Back Home

We were in Bloomington less than a year when Junior interviewed for a job in the RCA factory. In the end, he decided that he wanted to move back to New Orleans. He missed his hunting and fishing and was ready to go "home." RCA had a place for him there in this new field. In fact, he worked for RCA in New Orleans for the next ten years.

After we were married, I hadn't worked, but after we moved back to New Orleans, I went to work for General Electric in their office for a while.

But moving back home was just a start. Over the coming years, the frequent moving never seemed to end. We lived in various places in and around New Orleans, then in two different houses in Slidell, then in Thibodaux, then in Houston, Texas, then back in Milton, Louisiana.

Upon first returning to New Orleans, we lived on South Galvez Street, and then on Johnston Street. Next, Junior decided that we should move to Slidell.

During our time in Slidell, we owned two homes. The first, purchased in 1953, was a two-bedroom home with wood siding. It had a kitchen, living room and bath, but our family was growing, so two years later we purchased a larger brick home. This one had three bedrooms, a large living room, kitchen, bath, carport and utility room. Both of these were new homes. Terry lived with us for a while in that second home.

Then it was back to New Orleans and Dante Street. Next it was Thibodaux, where we lived on the corner of LA 1 and St. Mary's Street.

From Thibodaux, we moved to Houston, but first, we lived with a high school friend of mine for a few days and then in a house in Harahan while we found a suitable place for our family in Houston.

Then we moved to Milton. And then the world seemed to fall apart.

Before moving on, I must mention another notable event. While we were living in Slidell, Laurel Lee was born to us (in a New Orleans hospital), on April 22, 1958. She was named after my mother. Our little family was growing, and, with it, our responsibilities.

Chapter 12

Mother Remarries

Not long after we left for Kentucky in 1948, I received a letter from Mother that she was planning to get married again. Her prospective husband was an Air Force officer named Larry Heaberlin. I hadn't even been aware that she had a special friend, but apparently they had been seeing each other for some time already. He would come into the café where she was working in downtown New Orleans to have lunch, and they began dating.

They married that December and got a little

apartment in New Orleans, and before long, Larry legally adopted Terry, and he officially became Terry Heaberlin.

When Andy was just five or six months old, I travelled by bus to the New Orleans area to see them. (It was the only way to travel in those days.) They were living on Keesler Air Force Base in Biloxi, Mississippi.

In one way, Terry seemed happy with his new life. He was a boy of eight or nine, and things were looking up—financially at least—and he had a father again. But he was angry with me for having left him. Later, his situation would deteriorate tragically.

Terry saw and heard a lot in those years. Both Mother and Larry were heavy drinkers and smokers, and because Larry was not a very nice person, they sniped at each other almost constantly. Some said they deserved each other, and I suppose that was true. Having been raised in that poisonous atmosphere, it was not surprising that Terry picked up many of those same habits and carried them into later life.

I have no doubt that Mother loved Terry, but the lifestyle she lived before him was not good. She and Larry loved crude jokes and saying hurtful things to each other, and, sadly, this is the way many of her grandchildren remember her.

When Terry came to live with us in Slidell for a couple of years during his high school period, he was like a different person. Junior was very fond of him, and the two of them did a lot of things together. During that time, Terry also developed a very close bond with our girls, one that lasted a lifetime.

After Terry graduated from high school, he received a music scholarship to attend Southeastern College (now Southeastern Louisiana University) in Hammond, Louisiana. The years he spent with us been very good for him. He loved to go hunting and fishing with us, and we went out on our boat every weekend. He never forgot those good times.

Mother was married to Larry for more than thirty years, and he was so obnoxious that Donna (Terry's wife) and I both dreaded being around him. He was very mean to Mother, and because they both drank a lot, it was a very unpleasant atmosphere. That's just one of the reasons I've always had such a hatred of alcohol. I've seen the terrible effects it had on many families.

For now, I had problems of my own to worry about. Things were not going well for us.

Chapter 13

The Beginning of the End

The beginnings of Junior's illness may have been what today is recognized as PTSD (post traumatic stress disorder), brought on by his war experiences. He participated in serious combat in the Far East. At one point, a hand grenade exploded near his head, and he was fortunate to be alive, but it left him with shrapnel in his head, lots of pock marks on his face, and a lot of haunting memories. But, whatever the original cause of his illness, it was worsened by his drinking, and it gradually turned into something much more serious. Eventually he was diagnosed with paranoid schizophrenia and had to be hospitalized.

His erratic behavior and his drinking often left us in financial need as a family. Once the girls started school, I went back to work at the Frostop Drive Inn. Then, in Slidell, we opened our own television and record shop, and I ran that, while Junior continued to do TV repairs for RCA in and around New Orleans. I didn't have a driver's license in those days, but I drove back and forth to work anyway. Later, I even drove a school bus to earn extra money.

Through the years, because of his drinking, Junior had many auto accidents, and what we experienced as a family when he came home from work at night was largely dependent upon how much he'd been drinking before he got there. Friday nights were especially bad, and we all came to dread them. If he was not home by a certain time, the girls would go to their rooms and begin to pray.

You never knew what would happen on these occasions. Sometimes he might come in and be very pleasant, but it was also not uncommon for him to come in and dump all the contents of the refrigerator on the floor or pull the chair out from under me and violently dump me onto the floor when I greeted him. There were times when he told us that someone was following him, and he began carrying a gun. It got worse when he began to hold the gun to my head and threaten to kill me. This, of course, terrified the girls.

At times, I faced him and suffered the consequences, and at other times, I hid from him. The girls remember some episodes that took place in New Orleans, but the worst began when we were living in Thibodaux.

Junior had traveled to the little town of Thibodaux a few times to do television repairs, and a man who sold TV sets there kept urging him to move there permanently. If he did, the man told him, he would give him all of his repair work. When Junior next got the moving fever, he decided to take the man up on his offer.

Thibodaux was not all that far from New Orleans (just sixty miles to the west), but it was a very different type of town, very laid-back, and everyone knew everyone else. The children loved it, but at times I felt isolated and far from all my family members. I didn't see them much during those years.

We started in Thibodaux with a small record shop on a prominent corner, and, when that did well, we moved across the bayou and opened up a three-thousand-square-foot show room filled with washers, dryers, recorders, televisions, radios, stereos and our repair service.

The business grew quickly, until there were three or four service trucks, with servicemen all dressed in matching blazers. I had my car, and Junior had his. We were doing very well, and the future was looking very bright indeed.

Then, suddenly, his condition, which had taken its ups and downs through the years, took a sudden plunge for the worse. He flipped out, leaving home, and we didn't know where he was for a while. When I finally heard from him, he was on the road, he was scared to death, and he had a gun.

I didn't know what to do with the business. He was the brains behind it, but now I was left with everything. I had to let some of our employees go, but we tried to hold on as long as possible, hoping that he would recover and resume the work.

Everyone who called wanted to speak with Sparky and didn't understand when we said he wasn't available at the moment. I had to send someone else to do the service calls, and many didn't understand the reasoning behind this, and we were unable to explain.

Eventually, Junior came back, but he wasn't well

enough to continue the business, and we were in a royal mess financially. He decided that the only way out was to declare bankruptcy and try to start all over again. In the meantime, we had to begin liquidating all of the merchandise in the store. Since he wasn't well, I had to make the decisions about what to put into storage and what to return to the owners who had placed it in the store on a floor plan. Anything already sold had to be paid for.

Not long after this, we decided to move again, this time out of state, to Houston, Texas. RCA was again offering Junior work, this time in that growing market, and it seemed like an opportunity for us to make a new start as a family.

We stayed with my friend in Kentwood for a week or so, then we found a place for the family to stay temporarily in Harahan while we got things in order. Then Mother came and stayed with the children while we went to Houston to find a suitable place for the family to live. It looked like a reprieve, a chance to get it all right, a chance for a new start.

Chapter 14

A Growing Family

Before moving on to Houston, I must relate several more important things that happened during the Thibodaux years. There, on December 6, 1961, our fourth daughter, Yvonne Marie, named for a dear friend in our neighborhood) was born. With four girls now, we thought we were finished, but God had other plans. On February 16, 1965, Lynn Adair arrived, also in Thibodaux. Junior named her Lynn after a man he did business with, and I added the middle name.

Those were joyful moments, but something very unpleasant also happened in Thibodaux that must be told. When Yvonne was nearly a year old, I discovered that Junior had been having an affair with my cousin, Dorothy, daughter of Aunt Catherine, and their union had produced a son who was almost the same age as Yvonne.

Dorothy was wild. At sixteen, she was already married and had two children. Eventually she had five or six. At one point, her photo was on the front page of the local newspaper because she had abandoned her children. They became wards of the state, until their father was able to reclaim them.

The child of Junior and Dorothy, now ten months old, was being cared for by a certain woman, but her husband would not allow her to keep him anymore. The reason she could not handle him was that he suffered from frequent and violent grand mal seizures. The Mayo Clinic describes this malady on their web site:

> "A grand mal seizure—also known as a tonic-clonic seizure—features a loss of consciousness and violent muscle contractions. It's the type of seizure most people picture when they think about seizures in general.

"Grand mal seizure is caused by abnormal electrical activity throughout the brain. In some cases, this type of seizure is triggered by other health problems, such as extremely low blood sugar or a stroke. However, most of the time grand mal seizure is caused by epilepsy.

"Many people who have a grand mal seizure will never have another one. However in some people, daily anti-seizure medications are needed to control grand mal seizure."

His name was Bruce, and no one wanted him. So now he had to come and live with us. But he was the son of my husband's infidelity, and so it was a very bitter pill to swallow. Within a few days of being with us, Bruce suffered his first grand mal seizure, and from then on, he had them almost every morning.

I had to take him to Baton Rouge to find someone who could do a brainwave on him to determine the cause. There a doctor was able to successfully diagnose the grand mal seizures and prescribe the Phenobarbital that could control it. It was a horrible-tasting liquid, and Bruce hated it, but without it, he would have the seizures. He took that medication every day until shortly before he began school.

Because of the seizures, Bruce was a very slow learner. He would eventually get there, but it cost him a lot. It cost us all a lot. His doctor told me that if we didn't dedicate special time to teaching him how to do each little thing, he might never learn and would never be able to function independently.

For instance, he couldn't put his own socks on, and it seemed to take him forever to learn to do it. Once he got it, he got it. Eventually he went through school and became an award-winning nurse. Left alone, he might never have become successful.

The other children thought I was mean because I wouldn't let Yvonne help Bruce put his socks on. But I knew that he had to learn to do it himself. They were almost the same age, and she would knock him down on the floor and snap his coveralls, but he would say, "No, Vonne! Me! Me do!"

"You can't do it," she would say. "I'm gonna do it for you." But Bruce was right. He had to learn to do it for himself. And he did.

At first, his learning process was sheer torture—

for him and for us. "I can't," he would say, but we kept encouraging him, and eventually he learned.

As I noted earlier, Dorothy, his mother, died young. Bruce had begun searching for her when he learned that she had already passed. Our already complicated life was getting more and more complicated all the time.

Chapter 15

Trying to Start Over

The house we found in Houston was lovely, an older home in a good area, with good neighbors. Although the very large high school there was a serious adjustment for Andy and Lillian, after their smaller school in Thibodaux, the other children were still young and adapted easily. Houston was just "home" to them.

Junior was back working for RCA and seemed to be doing better, and I was relieved. Maybe we *could* make a fresh start of things and succeed as a family.

I enjoyed my walks in the neighborhood. Having been raised in New Orleans, I loved large cities, and I especially loved Houston.

Our house was on Haver Street, just a few blocks off of Westheimer and Montrose, and that was a place for art shops and artists, etc. In short, it was a very lively place, after having spent some years in a small town like Thibodaux.

I could have lived in Houston the rest of my life and been happy. But, as always, it was not to be. Things were not going well for Junior in his work, and he was having thoughts of returning to Louisiana. How I hated that idea!

Chapter 16

One More Try

We now put our hopes on the little town of Milton, Louisiana as being the place of recovery for us as a family. A furniture store in nearby Lafayette told Junior they would give him all their TV repair calls, and this gave us the hope of being able to make a fresh start. We found a nice house in Milton to rent.

It was an older house, but it was large, so we would have lots of room. There was a paved drive-way, and Junior built himself a shop at the end of it. The house had a nice front porch, a nice large yard, three bedrooms, a living room, a large kitchen, hall, den, and an extra-large room at the rear. In time, I would start grooming dogs in that large room at the back.

We make some decisions in life that we look back on and wonder if they were the best that we could have done. One of the decisions I made while we were living in Milton certainly ranks up there with some of the most difficult I ever had to make. Junior's illness had reached the point that it was unbearable, for me and for the children. He was out of control, drinking and threatening us nearly constantly, until eventually I reached my limits of endurance and had him committed. The culprit that caused it, again, was drink.

His slide into the pit was terrible to watch. In order to reach the people in their homes to do the TV repairs, he was working a late schedule, noon until nine in the evening, and since it was so late already, that gave him the perfect excuse not to come home until the wee hours of the morning, and, instead, to go to a bar and drink.

Many times he would call me at strange hours and say something like, "I can't come home because they're after me."

"Oh," I would respond, "who's after you?"

"I can't tell you who's after me," he would answer.

"Well, can you at least tell me where you are?" I would ask.

"Oh, no!" he would say, "I can't tell you where I am." And that was that.

Several hours later, he might come home, but he would be angry and throwing temper tantrums of one kind or another and making life miserable.

"Isn't it a nice day," I might say to him.

"No, it certainly isn't a nice day," he would reply and go off into some tantrum.

Amazingly, for the most part, he was able to keep his anger under control around the people he worked with, so that they thought he was a perfectly normal and wonderful man. They, no doubt, noticed his quirkiness at times, but they had no idea that he was so very difficult around the people he loved. His own mother couldn't believe that he was so out of control that he was a danger to his family and she, therefore, didn't understand it when I had him committed.

After he had been in the hospital for six weeks, I was at the welfare office one day, applying for family assistance, and when I got home, there he was. His mother had gone to the hospital to visit him, and he had convinced her to sign him out, against the advice of the attending physician. Of course, she didn't take him to live with her. She brought him back for me to take are of.

He was no longer able to work, and I had to get serious about the dog breeding and grooming business so that we could have food on the table. Eventually he got a little help from the Veteran's Administration, but he drank it all up, and there was nothing left for the family. It was all downhill from there. He was committed several times in those years, but nothing seemed to help him. He grew increasingly violent, increasing angry and increasingly aggressive. And he made my life and the lives of the children a living hell.

This isn't to say that every day was a bad one. When he was on his medications, he did well. He enjoyed life, and I and the children loved to be around him. But, invariably, he would get off of the medications, and when he did, it wasn't long before he was back to drink and back to his unpredictable ways.

Eventually, I just couldn't handle this anymore. I had children to raise and a business to run to feed them, and I couldn't be dealing with the constant tantrums and erratic behavior of a man who was not able or willing to help us. He had been very young when this all started (in his thirties), and he had grown increasingly worse. This had now been going on for twenty-seven years. If I had found some way to help him, it might have been a very different story, but that was not the case. Nothing seemed to help. In the end, for my own sanity and the welfare of the children, I felt compelled to seek a divorce. My husband was like a big, unruly kid, and I just couldn't handle him anymore.

Even after the divorce had become final, he kept calling me at all hours of the day and night, with his erratic conversations and his unbelievable demands. I often despaired of being able to continue raising the children and running the business because he kept us on pins and needles constantly.

Eventually he married again, an older woman, but the marriage was not successful, and his life spiraled downward. In time, he was found by his brother Norval living on the streets. Norval got him his VA check and got him set up in an apartment, but he kept drinking up his money and going back to the streets.

At one point, Norval couldn't find him for the longest time. When he was able to locate him, Junior was in a hospital. He had been mugged and robbed on the street. This happened a second time, and this time he lost a leg because of being drunk and passed out on a street where vehicular traffic was heavy.

By this time Andy and Lillian were gone from home, but I still had three of my own girls, Lee, Yvonne, and Lynn, and I had Bruce. My hands were full—to say the least.

Each of the children had their own horror stories to tell about their father and his drunken antics. Sometimes what he did was just embarrassing or troublesome, but sometimes it was damaging to them. He loved them dearly, but his sickness would not permit him to be a proper father to them.

Fortunately, before Junior died, Andy was able to lead him to the Lord, and he died in the care of a nice nursing home in Plaquemine, where the children had been visiting him regularly. It was a fairly happy ending to a very painful and destructive saga.

Caring for five children in the best of times is not an easy task, so I had all that I could handle, and, as much as we regretted it, life forced us to move on.

Chapter 17

Breeding and Grooming Dogs

I had loved dogs from a very early age, and we'd had one now and then, collies and cocker spaniels mostly, but they were just family pets. I didn't actually own a dog of my own until we moved to Thibodaux. Then Mother gave me a little Chihuahua.

There was something very special about having your own dog. It was someone you could love and someone who would love you in return. That began a long-time love affair with dogs, one that would prove to be a lifesaver—literally.

While we were living in Thibodaux, I began reading about a new breed of dog that was rapidly gaining popularity. They were called miniature schnauzers, and they were still very rare in our part of the country. I decided that I wanted one, and I looked until I found one I could afford.

As it turned out, schnauzers were very difficult to keep properly groomed, and because no one in the area knew how to do it, I had to learn for myself. So now I had a valuable schnauzer, and I knew how to groom her. My goal from the start had been to breed her and earn from the sale of the pups. That goal was not immediately met, but we liked the breed so much that we bought a second one and then a third.

When we moved to Houston, we had three valuable dogs, but someone there knew their value too, because before long, the dogs were stolen from the yard of our house. I was heartsick, and over the next several months, I kept calling the police and inquiring and listening to radio announcements about stray dogs until eventually I was able to recover all three of them. I always thought it was because schnauzers are so yappy and feisty that the new owners probably couldn't stand to have them around.

The third dog turned up in a local animal shelter,

and I heard about it on the radio. She still had a collar on. If the owner could describe her, the announcer said, they could have her back. I called immediately and described the dog, and we were allowed to go pick her up.

Later, in Milton, when Junior's mental state deteriorated to the point that he could no long work, those dogs became our lifeline. We bred one of them, and the first litter sold quickly.

At first, prospective buyers were a little reluctant, being unfamiliar with the breed and worried that they couldn't keep up with the grooming. "If you'll buy the puppy," I assured them, "I will groom it for you." And that was the way I sold my first pups and the way I got started in professional grooming. The business was a godsend. We needed some way to support our family, and this proved to be it.

Before long, however, I began to wonder just what I had promised. I had some simple equipment I used for grooming my own dogs, but if I was to groom many dogs, I would definitely need much more. We didn't have any professional driers, and we didn't have a proper raised tub for bathing the dogs.

Fortunately, we had that extra room at the back of the Milton house. It had been designed as a kitchen, and I was using it as a laundry room, but it was large enough that I could convert it into a place to groom the dogs that came to us now for this service. Before long I was picking dogs up from their owners, grooming them, and then returning them to their homes. And we had food on our table.

In time, I branched out from schnauzers to bloodhounds, and they were even more lucrative. In the last litter I had, there were fourteen puppies, and I sold every single one of them. That gave me money to do what had to be done in the months ahead. I needed a separation agreement and then a divorce, and eventually I needed to move to larger facilities. The sale of those bloodhounds kept us all alive for many a day.

Chapter 18

Surviving a Serious Back Injury

When Junior and I separated, we had a van and a station wagon. He kept the van, and I kept the station wagon because I knew I could pay the note, and he wouldn't be able to. He called me one day and asked to use the station wagon to go to Baton Rouge for an important appointment. I was very reluctant. He had a terrible driving record, and if he was drinking (and he often was), anything could happen.

"I know you don't trust me to bring it back," he said, "so come and go with me. I really need to do this." I reluctantly agreed. On the way back into Lafayette that day, a lady ran a stop sign and pulled out in front of Junior, and he crashed into her at high speed. Her car spun around and violently struck my side of the vehicle, and I suffered injuries to my face, knees and back.

My side of the car was so impacted that the emergency workers had to take me out the driver's side under the steering wheel. The doctors in the emergency room stitched up my face the best they could, but I would need plastic surgery on my lower lip and there was no neurosurgeon in Lafayette. And there was little they could do for my back. It would need serious surgery. I returned home, but two weeks later, I would have to go to Houston for the needed surgery.

Junior called Andy, who was living in Thibodaux at the time, and got her to come (with her small children) and stay in the house and look after her siblings while I was in the hospital. It took me some time to recover. When I got home, Junior had taken it upon himself to move back into the house. That didn't last long.

The accident left me with some permanent back problems, problems that complicated my work. But the work had to be done. I gritted my teeth and kept working. I had no choice.

Eventually the back healed, but it was never quite the same again and would often cause me problems in the years to come.

Chapter 19

Working with Show Dogs

As a dog lover, and now a dog breeder and groom-er, I began attending dog shows and got interested in training and showing dogs of my own. Working with show dogs is not for everyone, but for those who love dogs and love to see them perform prop-erly, it is a highlight.

Showing a dog is not just exhibiting a lovely animal. Everything that is done is governed by standards set by the American Kennel Association. Each dog has to be the right size, but it also has to be "well put together." Through the years, I won some championships and titles, particularly in obedience training, which became my specialty.

I was working on becoming a licensed judge, and although I never got quite that far, I did judge at a lot of local shows and fun matches, always in my areas of expertise—obedience and confirmation.

In order to become a judge licensed by the national council, you must complete a certain number of judging assignments, and you have to specialize in a few breeds. I was working with schnauzers (among several breeds), and while I was doing that, I also had to breed those particular dogs and become a breeder of record, and show them and become a showman of record. I was working hard toward finalizing my license.

I can't remember exactly how I got started breeding bloodhounds, but it was very profitable. My first bloodhound was a bitch named Saffire. When she began to produce puppies, I somehow got connected with the Louisiana State Penitentiary at Angola, at one time even using one of their studs. I was told that I was the first white woman ever allowed to go inside their kennels. They didn't allow anyone else to get close to their dogs, but they trusted me. The last time I went there with some bloodhound puppies for them, they told me that one of my hounds had been out that day in search of an escaped prisoner and had caught him.

Aside from the prison, I sold many bloodhounds to hunters. Those puppies sold faster than any other breed I ever raised. I don't know how the market is these days for bloodhounds, but for a while there, that was my lifeline.

Some Old Family Photos

At about 3

At a Mardi Gras ball

At about 8 years old

With another outfit

Mother

With Terry

Terry

Mère

Aunt Helen

Uncle Lenny and Aunt Margaret

Mother

Aunt Margaret

Richard and Gerry

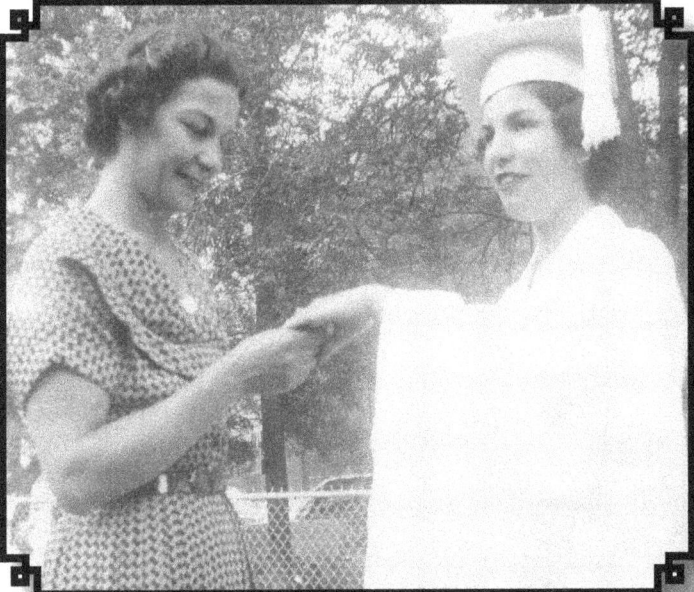
Aunt Helen (with Shirley) just before she died

With my five girls
From left to right, Yvonne, Lillian, Andy, Lee and Lynn

With Roger

With children and grandchildren about 1993

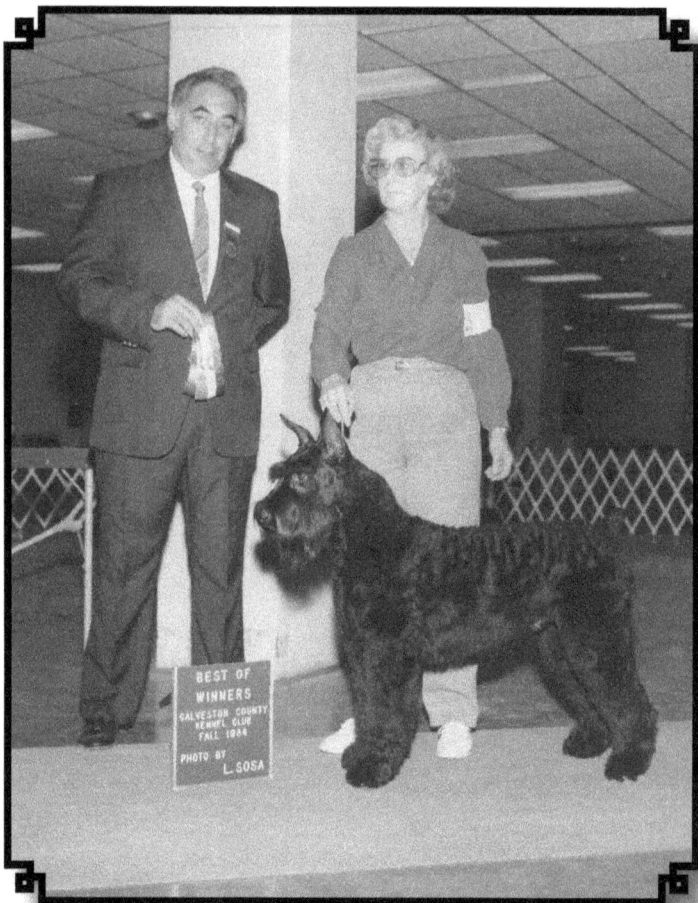

With my champion giant schnauzer, Tiger

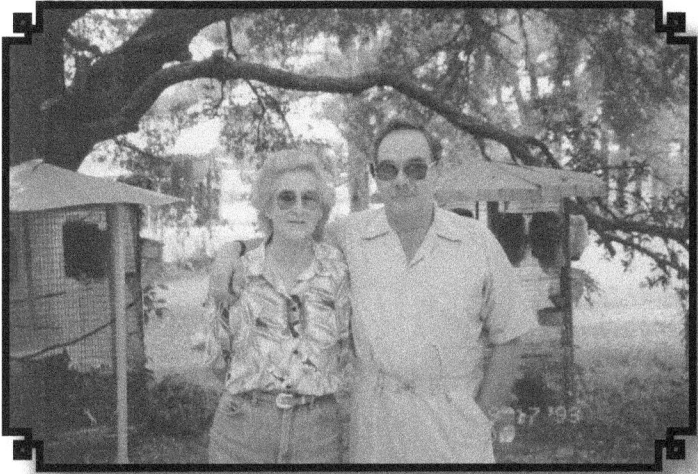

With some of the bird cages

Chapter 20

Moving into Larger Facilities

After many years in Milton, for several reasons, I decided to move to Lafayette. For one thing, Milton was far enough out of town that it sometimes seemed inconvenient for people to come out there with their dogs. Also the business was growing, and it was difficult to do all that we needed to do in such a small space. Finally, there were now many bad memories attached to the house in Milton, so while Junior was hospitalized, I took the opportunity to lease some kennels on the north side of Lafayette and moved there.

A lady who worked there had purchased and moved a mobile home onto the property, and then she was unable to make the payments, so I bought it. I made an agreement with the owner of the land to pay him a percentage of my income from the kennels. We lived there for the next four years and operated a successful kennel business, including breeding, selling and grooming dogs.

Then, one day, out of the blue, after we had been living there that long and operating our kennel business, the owner came to see me. He said that he had tried to sell the property and had been unsuccessful, so he needed to come back and work the business to make a go of it. He gave me thirty days to find another place. What were we to do now? It would not be easy to find a place suitable for this type of business.

Chapter 21

The Move to Gloria Switch

Some friends of mine, Elmer and Patty Kibbie, agreed to help me look for a suitable place for us to live and work, and I started looking too. It was Patty who found a property that had a house, a barn and another outbuilding on seven acres of land. It was located on Gloria Switch Road. It seemed to have a lot of possibilities and it was, she said, for sale by owner.

"But I'm not in a position to buy a place like that," I told her.

"Well, it can't hurt to go take a look at it," she suggested.

I looked the place over and could see that she was right. You could do a lot there. The house was simple, but it had three bedrooms, and the outbuildings could be configured to do almost anything. It was far enough out of town to be not as expensive as other, similar properties and yet close enough to make a decent business location.

I spoke with the owner and asked him if he might be willing to do some sort of owner financing or lease-purchase agreement. He said, yes, that he would do a rent-to-buy agreement. He would need eight thousand dollars down, and the monthly note would be a thousand dollars. Of that, six hundred would be put into escrow toward the purchase of the property, and four hundred would be for rent.

He had one important stipulation: "If you change your mind about buying and move, everything will have to be returned to its original condition." I agreed. The property had what I needed, and I had no plan to move again. I would use that property to meet my needs for the foreseeable future. It would be a lot of hard work, but I was accustomed to that.

It would also be a lot of expense. The barn needed many changes to make it suitable for a dog kennel.

I would have to borrow money to do the needed work. We had to pour concrete floors for the dog runs, put in drainage and a septic system for that back area so that the runs could be hosed down, and we had to supply the barn (which was quite a distance from the house) with water. Then, I had to fence in the entire seven-acre property. As the work progressed, every day, it seemed, I had to go borrow more money for something else, until I despaired of ever finishing the work and repaying the loans.

Within thirty days, the work was all finished, and we were ready to move. Elmer, who worked for an electric company, had worked tirelessly on the place in the evenings. He had divided the open area of the barn, raised up the existing bathtub in the out-building so that I could reach the dogs, doing the necessary carpentry and plumbing work. If it hadn't been for the help of the Kibbies, I don't know how I would have ever gotten it done and gotten it done on time.

They say that people come into your life because you need them. That was certainly true of Elmer and Patty Kibbie. All too soon, their own lives would end, but they had been sent to me in a very critical time.

Now I had a house, a barn, an outbuilding and

seven acres of land to care for, and I had to keep my business going and take care of my family at the same time.

Sometimes I had as many as forty dogs to tend to over the weekend. Every morning, even before daylight, I was out there taking dogs out, hosing out their runs, feeding them and exercising them. And then they would need feeding again in the evening. Often they also had to be groomed and bathed. The work was seven days a week, and we worked from sunup to sundown. Sometimes I had a hired groomer and bather and some kennel help, but the girls and I did as much of the work as we could.

When we moved to the new property, the transition was seamless. We told people who left dogs to be boarded and groomed, "When you come to pick up your dog, don't come here. We'll be in our new location," and we told them how to get there. Even with the move, we didn't miss a single day's work. We couldn't afford to. Every day was crucial. Friends helped us, and we hired a mover for the larger furniture, but we concentrated on keeping the business going forward.

Within five years, I converted the Gloria Switch note to a lease-purchase agreement, and the monthly payment went up to $1600.00 a month. By the mid

1980s I had paid the house and land off and owned it free and clear. We had done it with the Lord's help.

Then, suddenly, change was in the air. Something more than dogs was occupying my thinking.

Chapter 22

Falling in Love Again

I had been alone for six years and wondered if I would ever again enjoy male companionship. The truth is that the work required so many hours every day that I had little time for anything else. Just surviving seemed to be my lot in life—at the moment at least. Then, on Mother's Day in 1980, Lee gave me a gift certificate for dance classes at Arthur Murray's Studio. She knew how much I loved to dance, and those classes led to other dance classes over the coming months.

Dancing did several things for me. First, I enjoyed doing it, and it was a great physical release, but it was also a great way to meet people, and just to get out of the house was good for me. So every Friday evening, when the studio sponsored a dance party for all the members, I went.

One evening, some of us were doing a line dance, while a few others stood around watching us having fun. After that dance was over, a gentleman approached me and asked if I would dance with him. His name was Roger Irwin, and he was an engineer. Originally from the Toledo, Ohio, area, Roger had moved to the South because he got tired of scraping ice off of his windshield. He was working as a consultant with Shell Oil and had recently been divorced.

Roger and I started dating, and things seemed to be going well … or so I thought. But it soon became apparent that he was not yet ready for a serious relationship. Although we saw each other now and then at special events, we didn't date again for six months.

It was some time in August of 1981 that Roger called again and asked me out, and we started dating. This time he was ready, and we were married that November.

My children didn't understand why I was getting married again and, to tell the truth, neither did I. But the heart often knows better than the mind. Roger took me places and showed me things I had never seen or, perhaps, never hoped to see. He treated me with respect and always with kindness and love. We haven't always seen eye to eye, but he has always been there for me and has always supported me in any endeavor I happened to be pursuing at the time. Looking back, I'm not sure what I would have done without him.

In time I learned that Roger had an amazing mind. He remembers more facts about all sorts of things than most of us ever knew in the first place, and he has a wide variety of interests outside of his work: pottery, photography, cooking, wild flower research, reading and writing. And did I mention that he is a great dancer? That was what made me fall in love with him in the first place. I now had a companion in life once again.

Chapter 23

Raising Birds for Profit

Another phase of my life began out of necessity. I needed back surgery again. I had suffered that serious automobile accident in 1971 and required major back surgery at the time, and now again, in 1982, my back was preventing me from doing my work and would need medical attention. What could I do? Would I be able to continue working with the dogs?

I was no longer doing the dog breeding because, with the boarding service we operated, I didn't have room for my own dogs, but I was very busy with everyone else's pets. I hired some help to keep that part of the business going, but I needed to find some less strenuous work for myself.

I was still showing schnauzers and doing the obedience training, and Roger pitched in and helped me with it. But he and I had been to a bird show, and I loved the exotic birds and liked the idea of raising and selling them. This seemed like something I could do as my back recovered. I bought a few birds and was very quickly able to resell them at a nice profit. So now I went seriously into the bird business.

Roger enclosed the middle portion of my outbuilding and my carport, and I put cages around in both of those areas and began raising cockatiels, parakeets and love birds. Eventually a large flight cage was built in front of the house to accommodate finches. Over time, I had hundreds of birds to care for.

Eventually I did very well breeding and selling birds. People were very eager to get them, and I seemed to have a gift for raising them. They became like children to me.

Chapter 24

The Development
of Birds, Plants and Things, Inc.

Not long after Roger and I were married in 1981, the oil industry suffered a severe setback, and overnight I lost fifty percent of my kennel business. There was such an exodus of oil workers from the area that there was not a U-Haul trailer to be found for rent anywhere. People were moving out of the state by the droves.

Surprisingly, quite a few of those oil families brought their dogs to our kennel, as if for a weekend, and then they left the state and left me with the dogs and the unpaid bills for their care. What was worse, I had to feed and care for the dogs until I could legally place them in other homes.

Roger had been working as a consultant in the oil industry, and when it suffered that severe setback, his work was also adversely affected. I had started working with the birds, but the sales were not large enough yet to sustain us, so we now desperately needed some other way to supplement our income.

We decided to try to take the birds to the fleamarket on Johnson Street to reach a wider audience and get more sales. Some friends and associates had puppies to sell, so we thought we could sell some of them as well. But could we find a booth? If so, it might be expensive, and we were just getting started and didn't want to put out a lot of money we didn't have. In fact, we found that there were no booths available.

We befriended a lady who said that we could sell our birds and puppies from her booth, so we started. Each week, we transported our birds (and puppies, when there were any) to the fleamarket and sold a few each time. The lady who owned the booth sold plants and knickknacks, and I saw that she was doing fairly well with it.

Then one weekend, after we had been working

with her for some months, she said to me, "Teddie, I need to move my sales to another fleamarket, so I'm going to be giving this booth up. There's a waiting list for booths, so I'm not sure when you might be able to get one of your own. But if you want to, you can just take this one over and run it." I liked that idea, so that's what we did.

The lady had built up a clientele, so it seemed wise for us to continue selling some of the items she had sold successfully there for some years. But, other than liking them, I didn't know much about plants, especially about buying and selling them.

I began to ask around and get information that we could use in the business. I found a wholesaler out of Florida that delivered exotic plants to businesses in Louisiana every Wednesday. The plants were already wrapped and ready for sale. I found Kentwood Nursery out of nearby Broussard that specialized in ferns. Other wholesale places had their own specialty. For instance, I found a place in Gonzales that raised the most beautiful ivies.

To handle these plants, I had to apply for a nursery stock license. I could neither buy nor sell without it. But I had never let anything stop me when I had my mind set on something I thought I should do, so I did what was required to get the necessary license.

I was very fortunate that I was able to leave a lot of my plants at the booth all week, and I took home only the plants that needed a lot of watering. The place had its own security, so I didn't have to worry about taking everything back and forth.

At home, Roger had enclosed the carport for the birds, and now we put some grow lights under there, and that's where I kept my plants. That's when we formed our corporation, Birds, Plants and Things, and we've been operating under that corporation ever since.

As the boarding and grooming business declined, the plant sales increased. The ones we sold most were crocuses, ivy, tropical and exotic house plants and ferns. People felt blessed to get them, and we felt blessed to have another way to keep paying our bills and eating.

As with anything else, we gradually built up a clientele. People came to our booth regularly asking what we had new or if we could get a certain plant for them. If we could, we did. It seemed that I was always in the right place at the right time to get a break in the business world. Someone must be watching out for me.

Chapter 25

Expanding into Pottery

Although we did well with the plant sales, one thing seemed to hinder some buyers. The plants were potted in simple nursery containers, and many asked if we didn't have some in something more attractive. This began our search for affordable and attractive pottery pieces.

I found a wholesaler in New Orleans where I could buy very nice baskets, but that still wasn't good enough for many. I was also able to find cheap and attractive plaster pots, but when the plants were watered, the plaster began to weaken, and the pots leaked.

There were some young ladies in the fleamarket who did beautiful ceramics. Even though my girls had done some pieces over the years, I had never done any myself, but now I became interested.

When I learned that there was a ceramics shop in Scott, not very far from where we lived, and that they were offering ceramic lessons, I started going there at night to take classes.

I learned a lot in those classes, but eventually I noticed that they were not going far enough, so I started going to Baton Rouge to a ceramics center there to study more. In that center they taught a whole variety of ceramics classes, but they also gave teacher certification classes, and I decided that's what I wanted. It would take six or seven months of doing four-day weekend classes, and at the end of each series of sessions there would be a test, but once you completed the required number of classes and passed the final examination, you would receive teacher certification. In this way, I became a certified ceramics instructor.

While I was still taking the classes, I bought a few molds and some slip and started pouring my own pieces, using a bucket. I was very fortunate with my first piece. It was a potpourri warmer of a style that was just coming onto the market, and it was suddenly in great demand. You put a tea light under it to do the warming, and I had a hard time finding the tea lights in Lafayette or Baton Rouge. The reason was that potpourri burners were selling so fast that the tea lights had sold out. In the end, I had to buy tea lights wholesale in bulk.

The fleamarket on Johnson Street closed, but I learned about a new one near the Mall. I poured potpourri burners all week long, and then took them to the fleamarket on Saturday and Sunday and sold every single one of them. When other vendors sold out of potpourri, the people came to us, but I didn't sell mine apart from the burners. So if they wanted the potpourri, they had to buy the burner too.

Pouring by hand was very hard work, so Roger got his money together and bought me a pouring table, and we continued to add molds and other equipment and to expand our selection of ceramics pieces.

It was time to get out of the kennel business for good. Lynn had been helping me, but she wanted to get out of it, and I didn't want to hire someone else from outside, have to train them, and then lose them the next day. I'd done that too many times already. In 1996, I started holding evening classes in ceramics, and the response was good enough that before long, we closed the kennel business down and concentrated on the birds, plants and things.

I noticed, early on, that when repeat buyers came in they always asked the question, "What's new?" Or they asked, "Got anything new?" Twice a year I did a serious cleaning of my shop and everything in it and, in the process, I moved things around. The next time people came in they were very excited. "Oh, look at that. You've got some new items. How much is this?" The truth is that I had it for a while, but it had been sitting in some other spot. It only looked new to them.

These reactions made me know that to be successful in ceramics I always had to have something new, and I purposed to do that. I searched magazines and shows for new items and then learned how to make them, so that I would always have something new. In this way, I was blessed to always be able to come up with something new that people were looking for, and so my sales only increased.

Often, when I heard or read about something new in ceramics, I traveled to wherever that particular type of ceramics was being produced and taught, and I studied it until I could master it. I was never happy just to paint a vase, for instance. I wanted to learn about each new product, what it did and didn't do, and how it worked and didn't work. That kept it exciting.

Because I was always learning new things, I also always had something new to teach in the weekly ceramics classes, and that made my efforts doubly beneficial.

I like new things, and others do too. So I made it a habit to phase out older items and bring in new ones. That kept the business fresh and much more exciting for everyone—me included. I would never have lasted long in a boring job, and ceramics, at least for me, was anything but boring.

Chapter 26

Surviving Another Serious Back Surgery

In 2003, I began to notice that something was happening in my back. I had been suffering a lot of pain, and I went for an examination. The doctor was rather alarmed. I had undergone back surgery three times already, and he was reluctant to touch it. But test results showed that my spinal cord was being pressed from all sides, and the conclusion was that if I didn't have another surgery, I might very well become permanently paralyzed within a short time. "But," the doctor added, "the surgery might not be successful. You might wake up without the ability to move."

This left no doubt. It was serious surgery. If I survived it, and if I was able to walk again, I would need many months of convalescence, and I knew that no one else would take care of so many birds for me, and do it on a regular basis. When I had already put the surgery off for a long time, and it was now possibly life-threatening to postpone it much longer, I reluctantly came to the conclusion that I needed to get rid of all of my beautiful birds. But the question was how to get rid of hundreds of birds in such a short time without giving them all away?

I had some friends in the bird industry, people I had been working with for many years, and I now called upon them for a favor. I told them I would like for them to buy the birds from me—all of them. I would give them a very fair price, but they needed to take them all. I had surgery scheduled, and I could not risk having the birds left for someone else to care for.

I told them exactly how many cockatiels I had, how many parakeets (I've forgotten the number) and how many finches (I had more than 500).

Thank God, those people responded favorably and did an old friend a good deed. The people who specialized in parakeets didn't want the finches, but one person came and bought all of my cockatiels, one person came and bought all of my parakeets, and another person came and bought all of my finches. They each got a good deal, but I was happy with it too. Since I was in that desperate situation, they could have pressed me for a much better price, and what could I have done? Within two days, all of my precious birds were gone, and I was free of that concern.

Of course, I had very mixed feelings about this. I had felt forced to sell my birds, but they had been my constant companions for a very long time, and it was hard to see them go, like separation from family members.

I made other preparations for the day of the surgery, for no one knew the future. Of course, many were praying that things would go well.

As I was coming out of surgery that morning, the first thing I heard was Lee's voice. She was saying, "Mama, don't try to move. Don't even turn your head. You have a spinal fluid leak, and they have applied a lumbar patch, but they can't say for sure if it will take. If it doesn't heal, you won't be able to get up and walk, and any movement in the meantime could jeopardize your chances. It's very important that you stay still." They had kept me asleep as long as possible, but they had to let me wake up sometime.

The doctors later explained what had happened. I had a bulge on one of my vertebrae that was the result of the very first accident and surgery, and when they moved my spine, that bulge burst. While the spinal fluid was leaking, I felt nauseated, and my head and neck hurt. It was surprisingly painful, and until it stopped seeping, there was no way to know if the patch would be successful or not. Thank God it was.

It took a while, but in time, the patch healed. The next time I went in for a checkup, the doctor was pleased. "I don't want to see you in here again," he said. "And for sure I will never risk touching that back again." Thank God I was able to resume my normal life. The outcome could have been very different. That event could have ended my life or, at the very least, my useful life, but since then I've had many more wonderful years. God does answer prayer.

The worst part of the entire ordeal for me was that I had to stay in bed, with as little movement as possible, until the spinal fluid stopped leaking. Only then was I able to get up. I've never been one for staying still, so that was a chore.

I felt sorry for Lee, who had been the bearer of bad news more than once through the years. She had a small motorcycle at the time, and she rode back and forth on that cycle every day from Baton Rouge to visit me in the hospital in Lafayette. As always, my girls were very faithful when I needed them most.

In time, I was back at making pottery and teaching my ceramics classes. I sometimes needed help with lifting and moving the larger and heavier molds, but one way or another I got the job done.

During those years Roger also raised quails to earn some extra money. So it was caring for and grooming dogs, raising birds for sale, raising quails to sell the eggs, buying and reselling plants, making and selling ceramics and teaching the ceramics classes, and selling in the flea market. At every juncture, we did what we needed to do to earn a living for ourselves, and we were successful. When one thing declined or failed altogether, we found another one to take its place. We survived and, in the process, found something we enjoyed doing, something that served the community and, at the same time, brought us personal reward. And that's saying a lot.

Chapter 27

To Move or Not to Move?

Although I recovered well from my back surgery and still enjoyed hard work, my children began telling me that Roger and I needed to think about moving to a smaller place. Taking care of seven acres was just too much for us. There was the lawn to mow, the leaves to rake, the branches to pick up, the nuts to harvest, etc. In time, Roger joined his voice of concern to theirs. He no longer felt capable of helping me much with the yard work, the constantly falling limbs, the constant leaf raking, the constant debris burning, etc. We needed to downsize, he agreed.

At first I resisted these thoughts. The move to Gloria Switch had been a good one for me, and now for twenty-seven years I had experienced a stable home, when I had moved so many times before in my life. At various times, through the years, I had said to friends, "You'll never get my fingers pried off of this place. I'll die right here. I'm not moving again. Period!"

I was happy in our home, and I had been happy there for many years. Why change? I didn't feel that I was ready to give the place up yet. It had been good to me, and a part of me hated the thought of not being there anymore. So, instead, we fixed the kitchen floor that had suffered termite damage, the girls repaired and painted the living room, and Andy and her husband painted the kitchen and switched out the sink and the countertops. We had a new refrigerator they gave us, a new fan in the kitchen, and things were going well. Why upset the apple cart?

Still, the more I thought about it, the more I realized that those who were speaking of our need to move were right. How many more years could I mow all that grass and tend all those flower beds? And forget about harvesting the pecans.

When I first moved to Gloria Switch Road one of the things that had enamored me to the place was the many trees around the property. They gave it such a peaceful look and feel. There were lots of beautiful oaks around the house, lots of pines lining the property on both sides from the road to the house, and lots of pecans on the back acres. Those pecan trees would load up with nuts, and when it came time to harvest them, it was a very big job.

The first few years I lived there I picked pecans like crazy and Lee drove in from Baton Rouge and helped me pick up pecans, and we sold them. It was surprising how much we could earn just by picking up pecans. As the years went by, however, those trees became a strain on my back (picking the nuts up off the ground required bending over again and again), and the time of the pecan harvest, therefore, became a headache, something to be always concerned about.

My friend Velma baked a lot, so then she and her husband Nelson began collecting the pecans. That way they didn't go to waste, and they didn't clutter up the yard. So we were both happy. But, after a while, Velma and Nelson, too, were unable to continue harvesting the nuts.

In the end, it was hard to get anyone to come on

a regular basis and pick up the pecans. It was hard work, and the market for them was not as appealing as before. I loved those trees, but they were now a problem, not a blessing. I enjoyed looking at them, but that was about all. Was it time for a move?

Chapter 28

Resolving a Serious Dilemma

Although I had returned fully to my ceramics business, it was increasingly difficult for me to handle the heavy molds and the large containers of slip. They had to be lifted onto the table, then I had to pour them, and once the piece was dried, I had to remove it and then return the mold to storage. It was a lot, and I could see the handwriting on the wall. It was only a matter of time before I would not be able to keep up with it all. I wasn't getting any younger. I still stubbornly kept pouring them, but I knew that there would come a time when I could no longer do it.

Fortunately, I felt sure that when that day came I would have someone willing to buy my molds from me. Phil and Laura Potter had been friends for some years, and we had spoken of the possibility that someday, when the need arose, they would take those molds. I could not expect them to pay a high price, but I could recoup part of my investment, after having used the molds for years for my own work.

Being able to dispose of those molds successfully was one of the greatest concern to me. I had known many people in the ceramics business and had seen a number of them come to the same moment of dilemma and not be able to get anything from their investment. Seeing them stuck in that position seemed like a tragic outcome. I felt sure that I could get something back, and my friends would get something useful to help them carry on their work.

I had been pouring for Phil and Laura and making lamps and bells and selling them to them at wholesale, and they then resold them at a market. Now they agreed to take all of my molds if I, in turn, would teach them how to do the work. We had talked about it back in 2003, and I had asked them if they would be interested in doing this if and when the time came. Well, it had come.

When it became obvious that my back surgery was imminent, I called them and explained my situation, and we made the deal. Phil came over, and I taught him how to do the pouring for the pieces they were currently selling, how to clean them once they were dried, and then how to fire them. Laura came to some of my classes to learn the decorating processes. Fortunately, she was already an artist, but she had never done ceramics. Once he learned to do the pouring, cleaning and firing, they began the processes of dipping, glazing, and applying decals.

There was one more part of the agreement. I wanted to be able to continue teaching ceramics, at least once a week, if I was physically capable of doing it after my surgery. They graciously agreed.

Chapter 29

Trying to Sell in a Difficult Market

I had three real estate people come out to look the Gloria Switch property over and decide if they wanted to list it. One of them, a man, gave me what seemed like a very low estimate of what he could get. Another, a lady, never bothered to call back with her proposal, and I should have known then that the property was going to be a difficult one to sell. That was complicated by the fact that it was not a good time to be selling real estate. The recession was on.

The third agent, however, also a lady, came back

with what seemed like a wonderful proposal. It did seem a little unrealistically high, but the thought of coming out so well on the deal was very tempting, and so I made the mistake of giving her the contract. I did ask her if she was sure it would bring as much as she was proposing, and she answered with full assurance that it would indeed sell for that price.

She seemed so sure of herself that we immediately began looking for homes to buy. We found some houses that needed way too much work on them, and we found others that were far too expensive. Nothing seemed to be perfectly suited to our particular needs.

I needed an office for my photography, and Roger also needed one for his work. We had children and grandchildren who visited occasionally, so we needed at least one guest bedroom. But what we didn't need was a lot of maintenance or yard and tree work.

There were two houses that we liked. One was near Lynn and her family, and that was appealing. Having small grandchildren at our age has been a sheer joy. But that house had been trashed and needed a lot of repairs.

The other house we liked was clear on the other side of the Interstate in the little town of Carencro. It had many good features, but it just seemed too far away. Plus, there were way too many bushes that would need periodic trimming. So, for the time being, we came to a standstill with our house hunting.

I will have to say that the lady who listed the Gloria Switch property did show it a lot, but she couldn't get even a nibble. After this had gone on for a while, I asked her if she didn't think we should reduce the price. She agreed to reduce it a little, but not much. I pressed her. "Are you sure that someone will be interested in the property at that price? People are coming out here to see this, but for that price, won't they expect to buy something more elaborate." She felt sure of herself, but in six months of trying, she got nowhere.

When the six months of her contact were over, I made the decision to go with another agent, and we began shopping around for someone we trusted. We settled on a lady who had been showing us some available properties to buy. I really liked her. She was much more sensible. "Realistically, to sell your property," she said the very first day she looked at it, "you're going to have to come down substantially on the price. You're just not going to get what she has been asking." That was fine with me. I had felt that all along.

This lady took the property and began to show it, not as often as the other lady had, but at least those who came to look were more serious about their intentions.

Chapter 30

Finding and Moving into Our New Home

One day we were out looking for a house for ourselves, and the seller happened to be the same lady who had now taken on our listing. We didn't like the house she was showing us that day, but she said to us, "You know the house on the other side of the Interstate is still for sale."

I was surprised. I thought for sure it would sell quickly. It had four bedrooms, a large living room, three bathrooms, a lovely kitchen, dining room and laundry room. And it had big closets. The large living room even had a fireplace.

The property had a lovely white vinyl fence along both sides of it, and it totally closed off the back area to give it some privacy and security. It had a nice wide driveway and a large carport roof in the back. And there was also a nice play area and a storage building.

Inside and out, the house had many extras. Most of the doors, moldings, floors and lighting were not original. They had been added, and they were very nice. The owner had been a manager at one of the home improvement stores and had somehow acquired all of these extras there.

It was pretty much what we had been looking for, but we had liked the idea of living close to Lynn and her children so much that, in the meantime, we had placed an option on that house on her street. It was exactly the same floor plan and the very same age as this one we were now considering, but it had been abused and needed way too much work to bring it up to the standard we would need.

We told the agent our misgivings about the

house, but she suggested that we take another look. We agreed, and she called the owner to see if it would be a good time to see it. He was there and said that he would wait for us.

We liked the house so much that we bought it. Within ten days, the papers were signed. The former owner moved out and we moved in.

During the next couple of months, we sold a lot of things and gave away a lot of things. We were losing the barn, the large outbuilding and the carport, and we would have to downsize considerably. It all got done—somehow, and we moved into our new home.

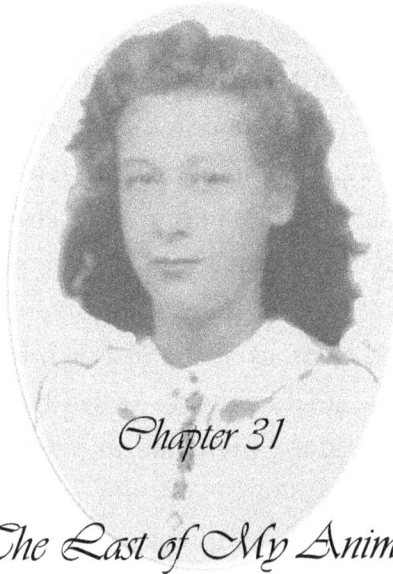

Chapter 31

The Last of My Animals

When I first moved to Gloria Switch Road, I had felt the need to get some sheep to keep the grass down in the back acres. Otherwise, I would have to mow it. The sheep were beautiful, and the children loved them, but every spring I had a hard time finding anyone to shear them.

I'd had no idea that sheep required so much special care. So I sold them. But that left me with the problem of how to deal with the grass on the back acres again. Someone said that goats would do a good job of keeping the land cleared and required very little maintenance, so off I went looking for goats, and I bought six and, later, two more.

The goats were great at keeping the grass eaten down in back, but they were terrible about getting out. And when they got out, they were very difficult to round up again. Oh, that was a lot of fun! So now we had to install and maintain an electric fence. That was the only thing that could keep them in.

I did enjoy having them. They were pets really, and I treated them as such. So when we got rid of the birds, the goats stayed. As we had been told, they didn't need maintenance, and they had plenty to eat back there.

Since the field where they stayed was just in back of my ceramics shop, I went there to feed them every morning, and they looked for me, running hard toward me each time they saw me coming. I fed them from my hand and talked to them as I did, and they seemed to understand me.

When it came time to sell the place, I finally had to get rid of them. When the men came to catch them and take them away, I was sorry to see them go, and I still miss them today.

I even had to leave my gold fish there, for I had no place to keep them at the new house.

Now I had only a few animals left. Sassy, our miniature schnauzer, had been with us for many years, serving Roger and I as faithful companion and guardian. During the writing of this book, after fourteen years of faithful service in that position, she breathed her last, and is no more. We still look for her each time we come home.

We are now left with two cats, Peaches and Abby. They meet me at the door each morning waiting to be fed. I like to think that they work for their keep, making sure there are no mice around the house, but Roger laughs at that idea. They're just cats, but they know our pattern each day and have made a path to where they get fed, walking single file in front of me Will these be my last pets? Probably not.

Chapter 32

Adjusting to Our New Surroundings

The new house was adequate in every way, but since we're all creatures of habit, it took me a long time to adjust to our new surroundings. After all, I had been in the same house for the past twenty-seven years. More than that, in the old place, there was always a lot to do, a lot of grass to mow, animals to attend to, etc. and so I went from always being busy to suddenly having nothing important to do at all. And every time I had to go somewhere, it seemed to always be on the other end of town—for instance, to my drug store, my bank and my dry-cleaners. Eventually I weaned myself away from that particular cleaners and found a closer branch of the same bank to go to, but for a long time, I went back to my drugstore—until most of my medications began arriving by mail.

I began walking every morning to keep in shape, I taught the ceramics class once a week, and I spent time with my photography, but I needed something more. Eventually I signed up for a weekly line dancing session, and since we had kept one kiln, I continued to do ceramics from time to time. Now it wasn't so much under the pressure of needing the income to survive, but wanting, instead, to bless my children and grandchildren on special occasions with something lovely and unique.

Roger continued to work as an inspector with a construction crew, so I was alone on most days, and visits and phone calls from my children became more important than ever. Someone has said that it takes a lot of courage to grow older, and they were right. Being busy is a lot more fun. I now spend more time with my photography, am currently a member of the Lafayette Photographic Society and have won some awards with my pictures.

Roger and I still love to entertain, and when

we have a day to ourselves, we drive around the countryside looking for beautiful things to photograph, and I've also had more time to reflect on life and share its secrets with you. Perhaps if I had been busier, this book would never have been written.

Chapter 33

Terry's Life and Death

Terry married Donna Cox from Jena, Louisiana, and, because of his work, in time they moved to Arkansas. They made a very nice couple and proceeded to have two daughters, Rachel and Rebecca. With that, they thought their family was complete. But, as we all know, the Lord always knows best in these matters. Ten years after Rebecca was born, Donna was expecting again, and Jeff was born. Now the family was complete.

For many years Terry owned and operated a

business in the town of El Dorado known as Photo Express. In that shop, he not only did development and printing of photos and enlargements for the general public, but he also did weddings, parties and school pictures.

When Jeff graduated from high school and was going to college, he worked alongside his father. They both became expert with the use of Photoshop on MacIntosh computers. Terry loved what he did, it was a much appreciated service to the community, and it provided well for his family.

When the photo developing business declined, he was still a few years from retirement, so he went to work in a local hardware store.

I am very proud of Donna. After her children finished school, she went back to college and became a teacher. The children who have had her as their teacher were very blessed because she loved what she was doing, and it showed.

Together they bought and developed a property in the countryside. They loved their trees and their deer and Terry even loved all the grass he had to mow on a regular basis.

Once in a while, Terry and Donna visited us, and we sometimes went up to see them. We also took a couple of vacations together and had a great time.

It was shocking, therefore, when Lee came over one day in September of 2009 to say that Terry had been diagnosed with terminal cancer and given six weeks to live. It was all through his body. He had not been feeling himself in recent months, but he was stunned by such a severe diagnosis. (We were all stunned.) In the coming weeks, he underwent some intensive treatments, but to no avail. He quickly weakened, and left us way too young. He had remained faithful to his Methodist church, and the funeral services were held there.

I cannot put into words what the loss of my brother meant to me. His coming into this world had assuaged my loneliness as a child, and now he was gone. It had never occurred to me that he might be the first to go. After all, I was ten years his senior.

I had experienced the loss of loved ones in the past, but the impact of Terry's passing has been particularly hard on me. I still have a husband, my children and my grandchildren, but Terry was my only link to who I was and where I came from. Since he left us, I have felt as though part of me was missing. Each day gets better, but the thought of him catches up with me at the strangest times and still brings tears to the surface.

He left me with some good memories, especially

of the latter years. He never knew a stranger, just someone waiting to be befriended. He could be obnoxious at times and, at other times, just plain annoying, but he was always himself. No matter what or who, Terry was unique. I shall always think fondly of him and remember the good times we had together

When Terry became ill, Donna retired from teaching to care for him. Then, after he passed, she returned to her duties for a while.

Shortly before Terry died, they bought a house in Hot Springs so that they could be closer to their children. But because he was so sick, Terry didn't want to move there. They stayed in the old house, with very little furniture, until his passing.

Donna now lives in the new house and is faced with the need to make a new life for herself. As for Terry, we are left with only his memory.

Chapter 34

Nothing Can Replace a Mother's Love

Unfortunately, my mother and I never had a close relationship like my daughters now enjoy with their children. We were never very lovey-dovey. Terry had a better life in one way (and in another way his life was a living Hell).

Neither Terry nor I was raised with either a loving mother or father, and the conditions we lived under would almost classify us as "homeless" in today's world. The wonder is that we amounted to anything at all in life. Thank God He was gracious and merciful to us.

It was frustrating to me that Mother never wanted to talk about the past and that she ignored my many questions about it. I'm sure it may have all been very painful for her, but I never understood why she couldn't seem to realize how difficult it was for a young woman not to know anything about her father or the circumstances of her birth. Refusing to talk about it all may have been simply a part of her nature; I'm not sure. But there were so many things that were never explained to me, and I never knew why.

There were other failures. For instance, nothing in my upbringing prepared me for life with a man. To put it very bluntly, I was never taught about life. Rather, I was left on my own to discover it as I could. As a young adult, I had no idea what family life should look like, as we had never had a consistent place to call home, let alone a normal family relationship. Instead, Terry and I were shunted from house to house and family member to family member, while Mother did her "thing," with no explanation and no apologies offered.

The idea of "my home" was a foreign concept to me. I obeyed the person I happened to find myself living with at the time and learned not to ask any questions, and that wasn't much of a preparation for having a family of my own. I think this also affected my children.

As I noted, in some of my early period, Ma Pool watched over me, but once I was four or five, I played by myself outside, with no adult supervision or guidance, and I don't remember her as being a loving person, at least not to me.

As I will note more in the next chapter, it was Aunt Helen who was the best positive influence on my life, and I was closer to her than anyone else. For one thing, she was only ten or fifteen years older, so she seemed to understand me. She was also kind to me, and that means a lot to a child of any age. Her care of me had to be a great sacrifice, for she had married young and had two small children of her own to raise on a very limited income. Logically she had to give priority to those children,

To be fair, they were hard times for everyone. The South was not very prosperous in those days, and many families were suffering financially. We had gone through the Depression and then World War II, and times were hard everywhere. Later, after the war, things did improve somewhat. Mother got a job for a while at what is now Avondale Shipyard, but when that closed, she went back to waitressing. But, although our economical status was somewhat improved, this did not better our relationship.

After I married, another element in my lack of meaningful relationship with my mother was distance. I never again lived in the same state as her. By the time we moved back to Louisiana from Louisville and Bloomington, she and Larry had been transferred overseas because of his work in the military. They lived in England for many years. Then, when they came back to the States, they moved to Arizona and then to the Mississippi Gulf Coast.

Somewhere I have a photo of Mother with a strange man, and I have long assumed that he was my father, but I don't know that for certain. When the Internet came into being, I tried to search for him. I wrote to a couple of Chester Burghers, and one of them answered me. He said he had been to Cleveland but he had never driven a cab and was not there in 1929.

At some point I just stopped asking my mother. She was such a hard person to talk to. I called her every week, and when I would ask her how she felt, she would answer, "I feel with my hands." That got old quick, so I started asking how she had "been." But our conversations were never fulfilling. It was always a struggle. She seemed to live in a different world and we had little in common.

I made the effort to go see her occasionally, but she never asked me anything about my life. She never knew about my marital problems. In fact, she never knew when anything was going on in my life, and that seemed to suit her fine.

The day I married Junior Fourroux, she said to me, "You've made your bed; now you're going to lie in it. Don't ever ask me to help you." And that was that. She never knew if and when I needed help, and I never asked for her help. Not even once!

She never knew when my children were sick. She knew nothing about my separation and divorce from Junior until it was final. I came to believe, in later years, that it was not just that she didn't like my choice of men. Rather, it was the fact that she didn't want the responsibility of knowing the problems. Looking back, it seemed to me that she had never wanted responsibility and had never taken responsibility. Until the day she died, I never asked her for a penny and never told her I needed one. She didn't want to know.

There was no animosity associated with this lack of communication, and there were never any angry words spoken between us. It was just the limits of our relationship.

While Mother and Larry were living in England, we corresponded, and she would send boxes of gifts for Andy and Lillian. Most memorable of those gifts were some very fine wool fabrics that I would use to make them clothes. Andy still has a sweater her grandmother sent her during that period. At the time of this writing, it is nearly sixty years old. Somehow Mother seemed to think more of the children than she did of me.

To be fair to her, I have to say that life, for my mother, could not have been easy. With little or no education, she had to make her way in the world without the help of a husband or father. Doing that is a lot easier in our world today than it was in Mother's time. Single parent families are fairly common today, but they were much more rare then.

Mother was always a very strong woman, not only physically, but also strong-minded and strong-willed. But while she and Larry were stationed in Europe, she started feeling bad, experiencing a lot of discomfort after eating. In those days, people were not as careful about their health, so it was passed over, and nothing was done about it.

When they eventually came back to the States and were stationed in Arizona, she went to a doctor there. The diagnosis was that she had carcinoma of the stomach and would only live six months to a year.

We were living in Slidell at the time (1958), and I remember reading the letter from her doctor. Without surgery, she would die quickly, he said. With surgery, depending on the skill of the surgeon, she might live up to a year.

Because of this diagnosis, Larry was transferred back to Keesler Air Force Base in Biloxi, so that Mother could be closer to her family. The military doctors at Keesler did surgery on her, taking out her stomach and replacing it with one made of sheep skin. Then she underwent radiation treatment. She was so ill that Terry came to live with us in Slidell and do his last two years of high school there.

But Mother surprised the doctors, living much longer than they had expected. They told her that she should just enjoy life, doing whatever she wanted to do. She went on being Mother.

In the end, it was not the cancer that eventually took her life. In the spring of 1982, she suffered a stroke that left her unable to speak or walk. Then she developed pneumonia and was put on a life-support system, and the family was called in. She was not expected to live long.

It was difficult to see my mother in that condition. What was worse was the fact that she had made me promise that I would never allow her to live on machines, if she had no hope of recovery, and that was the situation the doctors now described to us.

I really didn't know what to do. That was my mother, and I was being asked to make a life or death decision for her. I called Terry and explained the situation to him, and his response was that I should do what needed to be done. It seemed that we had no choice. Mother didn't want to live like that, and the doctors said that her hopes of recovering and living a normal life were next to zero. Reluctantly, we agreed for the machines to be turned off, and she passed within minutes.

This book is being written in September of 2010, and that is nearly thirty years ago, but I still miss her today. We had never been close, as some mothers and daughters are, but I loved her very much nevertheless. She was my mother, and each of us has only one. All too soon, they are taken from us, and everyone agrees that it is one of life's most traumatic experiences.

Being a good mother is not easy, and I know that I have made my share of mistakes through the years. However, I am very proud of the fact that I kept our family together in such difficult times and never abandoned my children. After all, they didn't ask to come into this world, and I owed them a chance at life.

Chapter 35

What Became of the Rest of the Cavaliers?

The rest of the Cavaliers, Mother's siblings, were very important to me in my early years. For instance, Aunt Margaret and Uncle Lenny were very nice to me, and I sometimes saw them or even visited them in Mobile in the summer as a teenager. They would take me to nice restaurants and to special places for sightseeing.

They also bought me clothes. Uncle Lenny's work

involved decorating display windows for shoe stores, and when they put out the new shoes, he made sure they were in my size (7 narrow), so that once the window was changed, he could give me the shoes. That kept me in shoes during high school.

Considering the times, he and Aunt Margaret were pretty well off. He owned a Cadillac back during World War II, and they ate out a lot. By accompanying them to nice places, I learned a lot about how to behave in public.

But, because she was nearer, I was around Aunt Helen much more, and, as noted in the last chapter, she became more of a mother figure to me than my own mother. I suppose Mother resented that fact because when Aunt Helen died, Mother, who was living in Arizona at the time, didn't come back to New Orleans for the funeral.

She did come back some six weeks later when Mère was near death. She had developed gangrene in one leg and had to have it amputated, and she was living in a nursing home run by Catholic nuns. But they had not gotten the leg in time. Blood poisoning had gone through her system, and she was growing weaker, unable to fight its effects. Mother and I were there when she breathed her last.

Grandfather Cavalier had passed away many

years earlier. He'd had a nursery where he raised plants, and I think this explains why so many of our family loved plants. As I walked down the street with Mère, she would see a plant she wanted to have and would snip of a little piece of it and take it home and root it. My girls do the same thing today. I was still just a child when Père died, so my memory of him is not very strong.

When I was a teenager, Aunt Catherine ran a lottery out of her house. It was what came to be called "playing the numbers," and, although it was a type of gambling, it was legal in New Orleans at the time. In later years, the numbers game came to be associated with crime syndicates and was banned. Today Aunt Catherine might have been called a bookie, but in those days no one saw anything wrong with it.

The wonderful thing about Aunt Helen's treatment of me was that her own situation was so very difficult. She had her two small children. At first, when I would stay there, I slept on a cot in a spare bedroom, and she made me feel very welcome. But then, when she had to leave her husband, his brother helped, by marrying her, but they lived as brother and sister, sleeping in separate bedrooms. He took the front bedroom, and that left only one other bedroom, so when I was there, the four of us slept in one bed together—Aunt Helen, her two children and myself.

Aunt Helen kept an immaculate house. You could eat off of her floor it was so clean. Sadly, she died young, at only thirty-six, either of a stroke or cerebral hemorrhage. No one ever knew for sure. Shirley was just a senior in high school that year.

Aunt Hazel also died young. She met with foul play. Someone broke into her apartment and killed her, and the murder was never solved, as far as I know. It happened while I was pregnant for Andy and living in Louisville. I didn't have money to travel to her funeral, and I was not in a condition to do it anyway. I had never gotten to know Hazel as well as the rest of the family.

Aunt Catherine died of a stroke, and I didn't know about her death for the longest time. It was Terry who finally told me.

Someone did call me when Uncle Gerry died. Then, I was able to speak with his daughter Jackie some ten years ago, and she was doing well.

Uncle Gerry loved me and my kids and was always asking us to come over, but Aunt Emily seemed to resent that because she had a child of her own, and she thought he should be paying more attention to her and not to someone else's kids. They lavished

Jackie with everything they could afford, but he was always telling me, "Bring your kids and come over. I'd love to have them." I could see that Aunt Emily resented that.

It seems to me that none of my aunts knew the circumstances of my birth. If they did, they never told me. So, until today, I still don't know where my name came from. Theodora is a very uncommon name that may well have come from my father's German community. I was told that it was Père who first called me Teddie. That name stuck, and I've been called Teddie ever since.

I've thought of looking up Theodora Burgher to see if I could find an ancestor I was named for, but I've always been hampered by the many different spellings of the family name. As a result, I have been left about as ignorant of my forebears (on my father's side) as a person who has been adopted. All of this didn't bother me as much as a child as it has in adulthood. At a certain age we begin to take an interest in these things, and since that time, I've had no one to ask.

It seems inconceivable to me that no one ever took the time or made the effort to invest in my life by telling me these things. I don't ever remember an adult asking me if I had any questions about my childhood or about how I happened to exist. Now they're all gone, so what can we do? There are lots of things that only God knows. Maybe that's how it should be. Who's to say?

Chapter 36

Always Wanting to Do Things Right

Most everything that I have done in my adult life was a response to the necessity of making a living, and I always felt that I could do better on my own than I could have working for someone else. If I had to go back and do it over again, I think I would make the same choice. It's so much better being your own boss.

With each of the businesses we owned through the years, I managed the office, the telephone and service calls, and did the bookkeeping, along with everything else.

Aside from the few other jobs I mentioned, I did work for the federal government for three years doing key punch work. It was for the early computer, called the Big Brain, and it was used for storage of data. It was boring work and not very fulfilling. The jobs I have enjoyed in life have involved things I loved and was passionate about. To work with something you love makes life so much more meaningful and fulfilling.

Whatever I have attempted in life, I have done with seriousness and dedication, never being satisfied to do things haphazardly or part way. If I'm going to do something, I want to do it right.

After I had gotten the schnauzers and learned to groom them, I began to get requests to groom poodles, but I didn't know the first thing about them. I thought of a young woman I had made friends with who was grooming poodles and wondered if she might be willing to give me some tips, so I called her. "Come by and watch me do one," she said. "I'm sure you can pick it up quickly." As it turned out, it wasn't as easy as all that, but I got some books and read up on it, and gradually I began grooming poodles too, and other dogs followed.

After I began showing dogs, I became a member of the local kennel club and eventually became its president. As president I held the first recognized AKC dog show (American Kennel Club for those who don't know) here in Lafayette and was President for the first recognized point show here as well.

The same thing happened with the ceramics club. I became a member and then eventually served as President of the club for twelve years.

If I am interested enough in something, then I'm not satisfied unless I learn everything there is to learn about it.

When something became too hard to keep up or something else was doing better, I changed. For instance, when I moved to Gloria Switch, I stopped raising my own puppies for sale. Then, before long, I also got too busy to do the shows. After that, the only dogs I showed were my own giant schnauzers. Doing the shows required a lot of travel, and we were too busy for that. Grooming and boarding took all of our time, and we just had to be there to maintain the business. One thing evolved into something else, and when one thing had to be dropped, I was too busy to miss it for very long. Something else took its place.

With ceramics, even after I became certified, I continued going to workshops. It was expensive, but that was the way to learn new things. And new was the key to growth and continued sales.

Things have changed somewhat in the ceramics industry, and there are other ways to learn now. But in my time, that was the way it was done. The point is that if you want to learn you will find a way to do it.

Not everything always went swimmingly with my endeavors. I learned to use the potter's wheel, but then, after I fell and broke my elbow, I was no longer able to work with clay. So I just switched to other types of ceramics. In a way, I was forced to do it, but I accepted it and moved on.

Nowadays, Phil continues to do the pouring and firing, and Laura is very good at painting the final product. They still ask my advice on many issues, and I help them all I can. I don't expect them to pay me much, but it gives me something to do, and it helps to keep my mind sharp. One day a week I have something to look forward to do, so I never die of boredom on Tuesdays.

I am not what I would call a master at Photoshop, but I have mastered enough to process, improve and print my own photos. And I often print for Roger too.

I even dabbled for a while with designing my own web sites. On one, I sold candles and my video on how to do raku. I didn't do very well, but I gave it a fair try and then moved on. Life is what you make of it.

I am blessed in that Roger has been very support- ive of all my interests, going along with whatever passion I had at the moment and helping me anyway he could. That means a lot to any woman, or any man, for that matter. Thank God for him.

My philosophy in life has been that if something was worth doing, then it was worth doing right, and I hope and pray that I may pass this philosophy on to coming generations.

Chapter 37

The Conclusion

So what can we conclude from all of this? As children, we had a hard life, but kids of every generation have a hard time to some degree. They didn't ask to come into this world, to live with this particular family, and there are lots of things they don't like about it, but they don't have a choice in the matter. I guess that's what builds character in us. We can either let life defeat us and make us bitter, or we can choose to make the best of our current situation and move on, hoping for better times.

All my life I found that I had to make decisions and then move on. Some have thought that I was hard, but this was the only way I could survive. Many decisions were made for me, and I had no choice. But whatever the case, whether I made them or they were made for me, I learned to move on quickly and not look back. Looking back is wasted effort. We can't return to the past and live life over. All we can do is try to live today the best we can.

When you hear words like, "You can't stay with me anymore; you'll have to live with someone else," what can you do, especially as a child? Something like that will kill you if you get too emotional about it. You just have to accept it and move on. It's not fair, but that's the way it is. So why worry about it? Life is too short to spend it in bitterness.

What happened to me (and to Junior) in childhood is the reason I was always determined to keep my children together. Children deserve better. They deserve to be raised by loving parents. That's the only way they can be their best. Why not give them a decent chance in life?

Early in life I learned to take people as they were and not to try to change them, and I think that has served me well. People are what they want to be, but we can't let that affect us. We have our own lives to live. Let them live theirs.

Because of all the damage drink did to our family through the years—my mother, my first husband, my brother—I grew to hate its evil effects. This should be easily apparent to us all.

In conclusion, life offers us many lessons. Whether we pay attention to them, learn from them and better ourselves is up to each of us individually. This is *My Life As I Remember It*, and now you have the chance to live yours. Why not make it the best life you can?

Postscript

I have often envied those who keep a journal. Years later, they can look back and have the detail of everyday life at any given point to refer to. Somehow I never had the time for that. Life was far too demanding. To get through the day was enough of a challenge, without trying to write it all down afterward. So there has been no journal to refer to. Instead, I've been stuck with my memory, and it may not be the best. But to the best of my ability, that's *My Life As I Remember It.*

Teddie Irwin

The Gift of My Girls

Through this book, I must tell my five daughters again that I love them very much. Each one of them has been a joy to me though the years. Sometimes in life you get exactly what you need and, believe me, I have needed the love and support of each of my girls and still do.

Andrea Louise "Andy," the first born, was a learning experience for me. A new mom must always learn all sorts of things, and I started learning the day she was born, March 10, 1949, in Louisville, Kentucky. I remember that it snowed that morning, and after twenty-four hours of labor, I was really glad to see her.

Being the first born, Andy had some privileges, but she quickly became a big sister to Lillian Ann, who arrived on July 23, 1951, also in Louisville. The two of them were very close, because they were each other's support system. What one did the other always wanted to do too.

It wasn't until April 22, 1958, when we were living in Slidell, that Laurel Lee made her appearance in the world. She took her good old time coming, and, for a while, we weren't sure she would make it. But she did.

Then on December 6, 1961, Yvonne Marie arrived in Thibodaux.

As I noted earlier in the book, with four girls now, we thought we were finished, but God had other plans. On February 16, 1965 Lynn Adair arrived, also in Thibodaux.

Through the years, my girls have been my pride and joy. Each one of them is special in her own way. Five girls, each very different and yet a lot alike. Each one of them has been my helper and my support. Even today, although they have their own families to care for, they are at my side anytime and for any reason I need them, even before I ask.

God knew what I would need, so He provided me with the undying love of five beautiful daughters. Thank You, Lord, for such a precious gift.

Andy is a minister and lives in Greenwell Springs, Louisiana with her husband. **Lillian** holds a management position with Sam's Club and lives with her husband in Richmond, Texas. **Lee** is a career military officer currently serving with the Louisiana National Guard. She and her husband live in Watson, Louisiana. **Yvonne**, who lives here in Lafayette, currently works for a Beauty Control consultant. **Lynn** and her husband live in Sunset, Louisiana.

Andy has four children: 1) **Patrick** retired from the Army after twenty-two years of service, but continues to serve the military as a civilian trainer in Kuwait. He has two children, **Pat III** and **Jennifer**, both currently in college. Pat recently remarried and he and his wife plan to settle in Denham Springs, Louisiana. 2) **Kimberly** has four children. **Amy** studied radiology. She is expecting Andy's first great-grandchild (and my great-great grandchild). **Connor**, who is finishing up his last year of high school, has recently enlisted in the Marines and will begin his basic training after the school year ends. **Aaron** is still in high school. He is the dancer in the family. And **Caleb** is still in middle school. Kimberly, along with her sons and fiance, lives in Indian Mound, Louisiana. 3) **Kenny** works for FedEx in Baton Rouge. He and his wife, Leslie, an RN at Woman's

Hospital, also in Baton Rouge, have four children: **Hannah** (12), **Sarah** (11), **Rebecca** (5) and **Luke** (3). 4) **Elizabeth "Lizzy"** is now twenty-seven and still single and works for the State of Louisiana in the Probation Division of the Office of Corrections in Baton Rouge. She lives in Greenwell Springs.

Lillian has one daughter, **Brandy Leigh,** and Brandy has two children, Lillian (12) and James (8).

Lee has three children. 1) **Teddie** (my namesake) is still single and lives in Baton Rouge. 2) **Jessica** married Robert Poole. They live in Denham Springs and have two children: **Madison** (3) and **Alex** (just turned 2). 3) **Rhett** has returned to college to finish his degree. He lives and works in Baton Rouge.

Yvonne has four children: 1) **Bryan**, who served in the Iraq War, now works and lives in Lafayette. 2) **Matt** is an MP in the Louisiana Army Reserves and is currently doing a second stint in Iraq. 3) **Nicole** has three children: the twins, **Christian and Athen** (6), and **Amielle** (2). 4) **Blake** is still single. He currently operates his own lawn service business in Lafayette.

Lynn has two children, our youngest grandchildren: **Ashley** (7) and **Tyler** (6).

Roger has three daughters—Victoria, Pamela and Deborah and one son, Roger, Jr. Victoria has a son and a daughter and one grandson. Pamela has one daughter. Deborah has one son and one daughter. Roger Jr. has no children

So, as of this writing, I have five children, fifteen grandchildren and seventeen great-grandchildren, and one great-great grandchild on the way, and Roger has four children, five grandchildren and one great-grandson. Not a bad harvest!

A Tribute to Our Mother

from Andrea Louise

In all of the world, there is nothing greater
than a Mother.
No position, no office, no title can come
close to a Mother.
Mothers deserve the honor that their
position grants them.
Poets have written poems, songwriters have
written songs about them.
God uses Mothers to help form us and to fashion
us into His intended plan for our lives.

And so we come forth as a by-product of their
love, their care and their leading.
Abraham Lincoln wrote, "All that I am or hope to
be, I owe to my Mother."
The earliest memories I have, from the time I was
about two years old, include my Mother ...
Watching over me, making sure I was okay.
I can remember my first experience of watching
raindrops running down the front screen door
where we lived on South Galvez Street in New
Orleans, and her coming into the living room to
make sure that I was okay.
Watching her make a homemade banana pudding
getting a scoop of it off of her finger,
and being able to smell Ajax on her hand, from her
cleaning the house on Johnston Street.
Standing on a chair in the kitchen with my
younger sister, Lillian, watching our Mother
peel potatoes.
Everyday homemade meals made from scratch
that helped to produce, in her girls and, now, in
her grandchildren and great grandchildren, the
ability to prepare fine meals.
Always a sewing machine and piles of beautiful
fabrics and trims to produce fine clothes for her
girls to wear on every occasion.

Always arts and lessons and crafts, and music
and dancing, violin and guitar, a microscope, and
stamps collected, and always singing together,
and a song in her heart, cleaning and cooking,
and gardens of zinnias and sweet peas, and
Christmases always filled with thoughtful
and loving gifts.
She gave me the wonderful desire to collect things,
and my first collection, at the age of four, was of
paper napkins and match boxes brought back
from her nights out on the town with my Father.
There was always a pet, a dog that eventually
would break our hearts by leaving, even a pet
squirrel that would play with us in the fig tree.
You have made us to be rich within ourselves!

Growing up, she was my angel.
And no one could ever say a word against her that
I would ever consider giving an ear to.

Mother, you have been our strength and our
inspiration in all things.
When we needed wisdom or direction,
we went to you.
You have been our counselor, our trusted
confidant, our prayer warrior, a peace maker, and
a forgiver of our failures and shortcomings.

Washington Irving once wrote, "When friends rejoice with us in our sunshine, but desert us when troubles thicken around us, it is Mother who will cling to us and endeavor, by her kind precepts and counsels, to dissipate the clouds of darkness, and cause peace to return to our hearts."

Thank you for being our Mother, our best friend and the person we cherish above all others.

Love Always,
Andy Lou

✠

From Lillian Ann

My mother, my friend, my mentor, who made so many sacrifices, who taught me to be an understanding and a caring person, who taught me to hold my head up high, to be proud and strong. But most of all, she is my Momma, and I love her with all my heart.

Love,
Lillian

✠

Mom,

As I go through my day, each day, there is always something that I do or a way that I respond to a particular situation that makes me think of you. And I find myself asking, "What would Momma have me do?"

There are many ways that I could say thank you for all you have done for me throughout my lifetime. However, the most important to me is that your strength, courage, your mentorship, and your unconditional love made a huge difference in my life. You are the most important person in my life, and I thank you from the bottom of my heart for sticking it out and for all of the sacrifices that you made and for being there for me. You are the reason why I am who I am today. I get my strength and courage from you. I hate to think what road my life might have taken had you not been there for all of us. There are not enough treasures in this world to repay you for all you have done for me. I do know in my heart that you will have many treasurers in Heaven one day! Mom, I love you with all of my heart!

Your Daughter,
Laurel Lee

My Life, As I Remember It

From Yvonne Marie

Momma,

I have so many fond memories of our childhood. For instance, it meant so much to me that you took the time to teach us games—like jacks, hopscotch and various card games—and when you could, you even played them with us. I remember standing at the stove watching you cook because I wanted to cook just like you. I always did love your cooking. I treasured the moments when you sat with me on the swing, and we ate milk and crackers together. School life was so demanding that those quiet times can never be forgotten. I might not have shown it at the time, but I loved working with you in the vegetable garden. That was an education. I kept bothering you to let me try my own flower garden, and one day you took me out to the yard and showed me a spot where you said I could raise some zinnias beside a pine tree. I've never stopped raising flowers since then. Thank you for enriching our lives with beautiful things.

Love,
Yvonne

I have many good memories of growing up at home with Momma, but one stands out above all the rest. Every Sunday morning, as we were getting ready for Sunday school and church, Momma already had our lunch in the oven, and the smells of it were wafting into our room. I could hardly wait to get back home and sit down to one of her wonderful home-cooked meals. Oh, that woman can cook!

Love,

Lynn